SPIRITUAL WARFARE AND PRAYER

BLESSED ARE THE WARRIORS THAT BELIEVED!

PROPHETESS **Debbie Jerido**

SPIRITUAL WARFARE AND PRAYER:
Blessed are the Warriors that Believed!
by Debbie Jerido
Fndforlivingwater@gmail.com

This book may not be reproduced in any form, stored in a retrieval system, or transmitted in any form without prior written permission of the publisher, except as provided by United States of America copyright law.

Unless otherwise indicated, all scriptures contained therein come from the King James Version of the Bible.

Published by: Foundation for Living Water
              Port Huron, Michigan 48060

Copyright @ 2014 by Debbie Jerido
All rights reserved

Front cover illustration drawn by:
Luke Richardson Houston, Texas

First Edition
International Standard Book Number:
978-0-9787585-8-5
0-9787585-8-7

Printed in the United States of America

TABLE OF CONTENTS

1	House of Intercessory Prayer	5
2	Apostolic, Prophetic Ministry	17
3	Demons, Devils and Need for Deliverance	33
4	The Stronghold of God	53
5	Travailing Prayer in Spiritual Warfare	69
6	Prevailing Prayer in Spiritual Warfare	85
7	High Level Spiritual Warfare!	101
8	Blessed are the Warriors that Believed!	115
	Appendix A	129
	Appendix B	131
	References	135
	Footnotes	136

ACKNOWLEDGMENTS

First and foremost I give thanks to my Lord and Savior, Jesus Christ, the Author and Finisher of my faith, the beginning and end of my journey. He is the Lord of my destiny. I also give thanks to my mentors. I have had some great mentors many by way of books, CD's, and DVD's. This book is dedicated in memory of the late Apostle Calvin Martin my spiritual Founding Father; to Apostle Veter Nichols; to Pastor David Nichols and NCLM; to Inez Robins a minister and friend; to my son Dale and all my children, grandchildren, spiritual sons and daughters for I love you all. Thanks be unto God: No matter what it looks like in the natural, even if you're facing Goliath, you are all blessed and on the winning team in this spiritual war as we walk by faith and not by sight!

HOUSE OF INTERCESSORY PRAYER

1

FOUNDATION FOR PRAYER

When we hear the word foundation one of the things that comes to mind is a building or some other type of project. We think of a beginning. In a building project the foundation is laid down first. Everything else constructed is built upon that foundation. So when constructing a project, it is vitally important what type of foundation is laid for the structure, strength and longevity of the project. If a builder uses inferior products and/or the wrong kind the structure will be weak. We can soon tell, in the years, to come as the building begins to topple. But, if the builder uses the right materials then a strong foundation is laid designed to withstand the storms of life.

Jesus illustrates in the parable of 'The House Built on a Rock' the violent storms of life can come regardless of whether you use inferior or superior materials. The storms of life come whether you use right, wrong or mixed materials. The decisive factor shows when the storm passes for the house built on the Rock Foundation will stand and the house built on the foundation of sand shall fall! And the Bible says Great was the fall of it! (See Matthew 7) In prayer as well, we have to consider the foundation. The following concepts may seem basic but I want to discuss the foundational reasons for why we pray. Many people of all walks of life and religions pray. However, I strongly believe a solid foundation for having a righteous, strong prayer life is to be a born again believer in the kingdom of God. After being born again the believer now has a mandate to pray at home and at church corporately.

The word of God says in Hebrew 10:25: 'forsake not the assembly of yourselves.' Speaking also of the assembly the scripture says in the book of Mark 11:17 'is it not written that My house shall be called of all nations the House of prayer?' So no matter what the name of the church is one of the foundational purposes God sees His church as is a House of prayer where believers come together for exhortation, edification, worship, instruction and corporate prayer.

Thus, believers have a two-fold responsibility when it comes to prayer: to develop their own individual prayer lives at home and the other one is to come together corporately and pray. For, Jesus said In Luke's gospel chapter 18:1 'men ought always to pray and not faint.' Jesus is the greatest mentor that ever lived and His life was an example of one who had a strong continuous prayer life. He commanded us to pray. He said in Matthew 26:41 'Watch and pray, that ye enter not into temptation: the spirit indeed is willing but, the flesh is weak.' Therefore, developing a prayer life is not optional nor is it only for the clergy. For God wants soldiers in His army. He has not called you to merely be a bench warming member sitting on a pew. God has called you to be a disciple a soldier in the army of the Lord.

We are in a war! We are not called to be spiritual jelly backs. We must grow up and become mature sons. I was born into the kingdom of God over twenty years ago. As a baby Christian I had very little knowledge of the spiritual war we are in. I was not as aware of what occurred in the spiritual realm when I was born again. A born again believer is a miracle—a work in progress as we learn to walk in faith like that of a child but nevertheless a miracle. As time progressed on this journey in the Lord, one night the Father told me in a dream: '*You are in a war! And you need to act like it!*'

When we were born into the kingdom of God we entered on the right side of a war, a spiritual war that manifests itself in the natural realm as well. For all war is connected to that which is spiritual. As we hear the word and study the Bible, we learn about this war. Revelation chapter 12 is very descriptive of the spiritual war we are in. The scripture says in 2nd Chronicles 20:20 'Believe in the Lord your God and so shall you be established, believe in his prophets and so shall you prosper.' We have to believe the word of God and stand in faith on it. His word is a weapon in this warfare. We must be strong in the Lord and endure hardness as a good soldier. (2 Tim. 2:3) To endure hardness as good soldiers we must develop our individual walk of obedience with the Lord, spend time in the word and spend time with God in prayer.

In this book, I discuss the different aspects of spiritual war and the weapons of our warfare which include Travailing, Prevailing and Intercessory prayer. All three methods of prayer intertwine together even overlapping at times to make for what is known as Spiritual Warfare Prayer. Often you will find that I refer to prophets in the book merely because I am a prophet. Yet, the focus of this teaching is for the believer and the body of Christ to better understand the violent nature of spiritual war and the dire need to learn to prevail in prayer.

There are different types of praying just as there are different prayers. Some basic prayers such as 'Now I lay me down to sleep type prayers', grace at supper prayers and other formal/informal types of prayers are good prayers too. But, you also have Intercessory Prayer with different types and different levels of intercession. The length of the prayer even as well as the intensity varies according to the church and/or the individual and what God is doing in their lives. A lengthy time with God in prayer can certainly be determined by whether or not you are called to be an Intercessor.

INTERCESSORY PRAYER

All believers should pray but some people are called of God to be Intercessors. An Intercessor is one who spends time with God in worship and prayer ministering before the Lord; whereby, you serve God with prayer and fasting too if need be. (See Luke 2:37, 1 Cor. 7:5) Anyone can spend time with God in prayer. Any believer can fast but Intercessors usually spend hours with God in prayer even days or more depending on the assignment. The Bible says in Isaiah 59:16:

> 'And he saw that there was no man, and wondered that there was no intercessor: therefore his arm brought salvation unto him; and his righteousness, it sustained him.'

In this text we see that God was looking for an intercessor and could not find one. Let there be no mistake about it, God is still looking for intercessors. God is All-powerful. He can do anything. But God has set up and ordained that men and women should pray and through prayer help to advance the kingdom agenda. If He doesn't find an intercessor, He is powerful enough for His own hand to get Him salvation. But we do not want that said of us as a church that He looked upon us and could not find one to intercede and stand in the gap. For, that is a sign of weakness. It is the will of God that we pray! God has not cast his people away. Intercession is made to God for his church. (see Ro. 11:2) That word Intercessor means intermediary, arbitrator, a negotiator, a Go-between, Mediator, Liaison or an Agent. An intercessor is one who takes the place of another and pleads their case, petitions on behalf of, stand between. We intercede to change the direction of a thing based on God's agenda, to see victory in the lives of people as well as the church. Intercessors also bear some characteristics of watchmen in that they stand in the gap and pray. Prophets are watchmen. Therefore all prophets are intercessors (have a prayer life) but all intercessors are not prophets. In the book of Ezekiel 22:30; God said:

> 'And I sought for a man among them, that should make up the hedge, and stand in the gap before me for the land, that I should not destroy it: but I found none'.

Ezekiel paints a sad picture just like Isaiah did because the lack of intercession happened again. God could not find a man to stand in the gap and take notice He was looking among the congregation not the world. God sent his son Jesus into this world to save men's lives not to destroy them. Jesus is our Chief Intercessor, the High Priest of our confession and the firstborn of the bretheren. (see Rom. 8:29) We can be thankful that God is not like man. He is not a respecter of persons. He doesn't want anyone to perish. Therefore we need more intercessors to stand in the gap—to stop the destructive work of the devil in the lives of people and win souls for the kingdom of God. An Intercessor—watchman on the wall, through prayer stands in the gap and pleads the case on behalf of the people, persons, entity or an individual. God said in the book of Isaiah:

> 'For Zion's sake will I not hold my peace, and for Jerusalem's sake I will not rest, until the **righteousness** thereof go forth as **brightness**, and the salvation thereof as a lamp that burneth. And the Gentiles shall see thy righteousness, and all kings thy glory:...' (Isaiah 62: 1-2)

> 'I have set watchmen upon thy walls, O Jerusalem, which shall never hold their peace day nor night: ye that make mention of the LORD, keep not silence, And give him no rest, till he **establish**, and till he make Jerusalem **a praise** in the earth.' (Is. 62: 6-7)

BEARER OF BURDENS

Intercessors are called upon to spend time with God praying until the peace and establishment of God's kingdom in the earth realm is manifested in fullness in their personal lives as well as the church. The following are some characteristics of intercessors to help you to identify if you are called to be an intercessor. An Intercessor is not one of the five-fold ministry gifts listed in Ephesians the fourth chapter; yet, it's a calling. Intercessors bear some similarities to prophets in that they may sense a burden of the Lord within them. This burden can also come from observation of the things that you see going on in and around you. (see Mark 11:11)

You can become weighted down by this burden experiencing feelings of sadness, sorrow and even depression. The burden does not lift until you pray through as those mothers in the church would say. Praying through means obtaining the peace of God no matter what you're facing. Some intercessory prayer assignments from the Lord can be for individuals, your church, souls to come into the Kingdom, your cities, nation and indeed the world. Standing in the gap as an intercessor is a process that involves helping to build and rebuild in the Kingdom of God.

In the **Book of Nehemiah** we read about the task he had as Governor of rebuilding the walls of Jerusalem. Due to the sin of the leaders, the people, and the refusal to turn away from their sins—the nation had been torn down by the ravages of war and burned by the enemy. The people (right along with the leaders) had been taken into captivity. Nehemiah was commissioned by heaven's throne room of mercy and grace and reinforced by the authority of the earthly King to help rebuild the walls and the city. Nehemiah described the burdens and the task of the burden bearers as follows:

'And Judah said, The strength of the bearers of burdens is decayed, and there is much rubbish; so that we are not able to build...' (Neh. 4:10)

As we read the book of Nehemiah we become more aware of how the enemy will fight the process of building and rebuilding. Because of the continuous oppression of the enemy, they had to build with a brick in one hand and a sword prepared for war in the other hand. As, intercessors the bricks can represent whatever our hands find God ordained to do. So you can be an usher, a deacon, or a lay member. Or you can be an intercessor singing in the choir. Singing in the choir is not who you are, it's what you do. You can be a leader and be an intercessor too. Jesus said occupy until I come. (see Luke 19:13)

The sword of the Intercessor, the Word of God, is quite an effective weapon to wage war with in prayer; to destroy the works of the devil by the Word, by the Spirit and by the Blood. The work of intercessory prayer is not always easy. Prayer is work requiring dedication and time allotted. This bearing of burdens through prayer can be laborious, draining work were divine discontentment sets in. You have to discharge the burden in prayer through the power of the Spirit. Even though it can be exacting, we are not wasting our time. God means business and we mean business with God by not being slothful and overcome with ease in Zion.

The responsibility of prayer takes place at home in your individual prayer closet and at church with the local body. In Haggai chapter 1:4 God said (concerning his temple) 'Is it time for you...to dwell in your ceiled houses, and this house lie waste?' God is not just talking about the physical structure of the building alone but He is talking about the spiritual temperature of the Temple too. The enemy fights prayer more than anything else because prayer is one of the most effective weapons, to demolish the devils strongholds and set the captive free.

WARFARE OF INIQUITY

The nature of war is complex. Intercessors must assess the situation for casualty, loss and damage control. Nehemiah's assessment concluded that there was much rubbish to the point they were not able to build. That was thousands of years ago but what happened to Jerusalem is still happening to the people of the Lord today. The war between good and evil rages on. Many times the intensity of the war depends on the level of iniquity, sin, witchcraft and idolatry involved. There are principalities and territorial spirits assigned to different locations that oppose the church. That's why we must be strong in the Lord and the power of his might. For as you intercede on behalf of the church, you are very well in a position to take artillery fire whether it be retaliation, backlash or merely front line fire encountered as you engage in war.

Soldiers know the battle can become severely intense. That's why we need more intercessors. It's not just souls that need to come into the kingdom but people can be snared right in the church, saved thirty years but sitting on the pew captured by a religious spirit. A religious spirit is one of the most diabolical demons you will ever encounter. The Pharisees, rulers and leaders walked in a religious spirit. This demon seeks to thwart the move of God. This demon seeks to stop God's work and advance its own agenda. A religious devil is usually well versed and knowledgeable of many things of the spirit. So don't be surprised. Satan quotes the word. Speaking to Jesus the devil said—it is written…

A very good source on this spiritual war we are engaged in is 'The Three Battlegrounds' a book written by Frances Frangapaine where he discusses the battleground of the mind, the battleground of the church and the battleground of the heavenlies described as the war over reality. All three areas deal with strongholds and spiritual warfare reinforcing the urgent need for believers to pray. This battle rages within the church as well as without. The battle can rage in our emotions within our soul too. This war in the heavenlies, is an unseen war—a spiritual war without hands. Yet manifestations of this unseen war are evident in varying degrees in our personal lives, the church and the world.

Satan seeks to divert the believer and the church from their true identity and purpose in God. Satan does not want us to know who we are in God or the power we possess. That's why the devil does not want us to pray. For, our authority and identity (which existed from the foundation of the world, sealed by the blood of the Lamb) is fortified in our minds and hearts through locking in with God in intercessory prayer. (see Ephesians 1,2)

For these reasons and more we must guard against prayerlessness, slothfulness, un-forgiveness, cold-love, distractions, diversions and detours. For when the war becomes intense, like that of a raging sea; tempers can flare and emotions emerge. You can end up feeling like there are '*two executioners both seemingly equally strong pulling you at the same time in two different directions.*[1] One major reason for this is because there is no middle ground in this war. Despite the circumstances you are either for Him or against Him. God is not schizophrenic. He knows He is on our side. Do we know whose side we are on when the storms of life violently beat upon the house? Speaking of John the Baptist the scriptures said what did you go out to see? Was it one dressed in fine clothing? They who wear fine clothing are in kings palaces. Or was it a reed shaken in the wind? (see Matt. 11:7-9) Perhaps it was a violent, vicious and wicked wind!

Jesus spoke to the wind. He spoke with authority to the raging sea and commanded it to be still! (see Mark 4:35-39) Whereas, the disciples caught up in the brutal relentless manifestation of the elements and their raging emotions, cried out for fear! Make no mistake about it we are just as human as the apostles. We too can get caught up in feelings and lost in the winds of emotion in spiritual warfare. Some people haven't been through much. They've never fought a serious battle but Job has. Though the storm may come and the vicious winds may blow we can stand in the gap on our own behalf and in the name of Jesus Christ command the raging sea of our emotions to be still! Command your soul to be still! Take authority and command the devil to stop manipulating against your mind, your emotions and your will!

In my book "Rivers of Waters: Pro-choice" a memoir on personal deliverance, I discussed the issue of being 'Torn between Two Lovers.' Spiritual whoredom, mixed spirits and gospel idolatry are just a few modern terms for this iniquity. These sins manifest in the natural realm as the battle for the soul rages on within and without. There are times when the severity of the battle can become overwhelming making you feel like you're sick! Daniel the prophet said he was overwhelmed and became sick when it was revealed to him the scene behind the seen. (see Daniel 8) The disciples were amazed as they approached Jerusalem for Jesus had told them what he was about to suffer. (see Mark 10) That word amazed means overwhelmed.

As spiritual warfare increases rebellion arises and/or as rebellion arises warfare increases. One night, I was reading the 13th chapter of the book of Numbers. The children of Israel like their predecessors in Nehemiah were rebellious and had sinned. As a result they were sentenced to forty years in the wilderness. The irony is even though Moses, Joshua, and Caleb were faithful they had to endure this sentencing right along with those rebellious people. As I thought on this, a strange, foreboding, eerie-like feeling came over me and that night for a good portion of the entire night I had prophetic dreams. God communed with me about Destiny which encouraged and strengthened me.

War is frightening to the human psyche and soul. War is devastating! Many times, we don't want to be conscious that we are in a war because war is not pleasant to think about. The natural man doesn't want to deal with spiritual war. The soul caught up in the paradigm of old thinking gets hindered by a spirit of fear. But we must be spiritually strong because Satan done counted the carnal Christian out! Whether we are war conscious or not the war rages on! Whether you own up to it or not, enemy tanks roll on with or without your presence on the battlefield. There is much casualty and loss if you become distracted, or diverted. The enemy wants you to defect so he can detour you from God's greater purpose and highest blessing for your life.

Then God has to put you back on the right track even in your mind. The nursery rhyme society taught the old mind was: 'humpty dumpty sat on a wall. Humpty dumpty had a great fall. All the Kings horses and all the king's men couldn't put humpty together again.' But the good news is: GOD Can! A made up mind is not enough. We need the mind of Christ to stand in this war. All truth is parallel. As in natural war, so it is in spiritual war. There are casualties in spiritual war too both physically and spiritually.

FRIENDLY FIRE!

One of the most vicious and devastating blows in spiritual warfare is friendly fire. Friendly fire is what occurs when the battle gets so intense the soul gets out of control and out of fear believers end up shooting at each other. The scriptures clearly tell us that we are not one another's enemy. The devil is the enemy! Satan accuses us day and night before God with legitimate cases. The devil is the Accuser of the Bretheren. (see Rev. 12:10) We must guard against agreeing with the enemy (through the spirit of accusation) against one another. That is why it is pertinent that we develop a strong life of prayer. Prayer helps crucify the flesh—the carnal thought life of the old man. For fighting each other is the mark of a carnal mind, sin and an un-crucified life. The Bible tells us that the weapons of our warfare are not carnal but mighty through God to the pulling down of strongholds. One of the main reasons for friendly fire is that people need deliverance. Many opposing forces of the enemy are at work such as witchcraft, jealousy, competition, corruption, sabotage and control. Though the fire is described as friendly it is highly dangerous and even lethal.

The fire is called friendly because the people involved are thought to be your brothers and your sisters in Christ. But just as in natural families so it is in spiritual families. We love our biological siblings and we have to love our spiritual brothers and sisters too despite what occurs. Who said love was easy? Who said love always feels good? Well, what's love got to do with it? Love has everything to do with it for God is love. Jesus commanded us to love one another, a love not only in tongue but in deeds. (see John 13:34) Jesus said this is how men know that you are my disciples when you love one another. (see John 13:35) When people don't walk in that love, the devil is at work and they need deliverance. Not walking in love as well as other sin is part of the warfare of iniquity. We will talk about deliverance in detail in another chapter. We must use our spiritual weapons of warfare including personal prayer, praise, worship and corporate prayer in the church to overcome in this war.

APOSTOLIC PROPHETIC MINISTRY

2

THE ASSIGNMENT OF CORPORATE PRAYER

As I stated previously, when it comes to prayer, the responsibility of the believer is two-fold in the prayer closet at home and at the church. The believer is strengthened as they actively engage and take part in corporate prayer. The Father showed me in a prophetic dream that in the body of Christ (in general) believers sometimes do a good job of praying in their individual prayer closets. However, they don't tend to do as well when it comes to assembling for corporate prayer. I wondered why? For various reasons of course, many people do not come out for prayer. Some have come to prayer and been wounded. The altar has become contaminated due to contaminated hearts and needs to be restored. Some people have a Sunday only mentality. Some people are intimidated by praying with others or fear praying in public. Some people are very selective about who they pray with. Some simply lack motivation and desire to pray. Last but certainly not least, many times the Sunday service is esteemed more highly, receives more reinforcement and is treated as though it is even more important to God.

Although I regularly attended church, I confess that years ago when God first called me to be an intercessor, I prayed less than five minutes a day. Due to this infrequent personal fellowship, my prayers lacked intimacy and worship. As, I said in chapter one 'in a spiritual war but yet don't act like it.' On the surface it seems I had no desire to pray any more than already did. Perhaps I thought it was only for certain members of the clergy. God had to shake me! After God called me to intercede, I began going more to the Upper Room in the Prayer Tower at my church. I also began rising up earlier in the morning to spend more time with God in personal prayer. This was a struggle because I was not used to getting up that early in the morning. It was also a struggle to go to corporate prayer because unlike church on Sunday the prayer meeting was not as predictable and I like structure. There were less people. Many times hardly any people at all. There was hardly any worship music if any making for a monotonous atmosphere. Also making you wonder if 'The Church in Christ' denomination had stumbled upon some dire truth concerning music in church. Thus at times the prayer service seemed dry, vulnerable to error and unorthodox.

Despite the lack of structure, maintaining corporate prayer is vital for developing strong churches with an apostolic, prophetic flow. We must stay focused. Apostolic is kingdom. Prophetic is prophecy and the testimony of Jesus is the spirit of prophecy. (see Rev. 19:10) Deliverance is seeing the captive set free and maintaining that walk of freedom in Christ. Our goal as an apostolic church is to demolish demonic strongholds and advance the kingdom of God: so that people don't continue to live in cycles of bondage and defeat; so that we are not robbed of our inheritance and find the next generation missing in action from the church.

We can't afford to just slip out of here on a banana peel singing lullabies on our way to heaven while our love ones and the world is dying and going to hell all around us. As a church, as a corporate body we don't want to live in cycles of defeat, a process known as demonic cycling. First John 3:8 says '...For this purpose the Son of God was manifested, that he might destroy the works of the devil'. God wants His people to live in victory. The enemy wants us to walk around defeated with our heads hanging down engaged in friendly fire fighting one another. Some strongholds cannot be merely broken in your individual prayer closet because when God saved you, He placed you in a local body—the church and whatever times leadership has set for services, if we can, we should endeavor to come out.

Here is a list of some strongholds that need to be broken: physical sickness, sinful habits, mental issues, premature death, constant financial problems (poverty, lack, debt) drugs, violence, serious trouble with children or other relationships. These vices can grip people even our loved ones to the point that they become casualties of war. That's why we need to come out for corporate prayer and pray. We'll discuss these casualties of war in more detail later. But first let's talk about the Assignment of the Leader, the leadership of the local body and the Intercessory Prayer Team. Their relationship should be harmonious. The Bible says in Proverbs 29:18 'without a vision the people perish'. Habakkuk 2:2 says 'write the vision and make it plain'. People naturally do not like to be a part of something they can't understand. So in this passage God is saying the vision needs to be made plain so that when the people read it, they will run with the vision—help to give it arms, legs, feet, etc. In order to fulfill the vision authority, order and submission are necessary.

AUTHORITY AND SUBMISSION

Authority and submission are widely spoken of in the body of Christ. However, you have leaders who want sheep to submit to them but they won't submit or be accountable to anyone themselves. Just as prayer is two-fold, submission and authority is two-fold. Submission is for the people in the pews and submission is for the pulpit too. For, there must be accountability and order in God's house. He commands us to submit to authority and despite titles and position, he also commands us to be subject to one another. (see 1 Peter 5:5) That is respect to the Christ in each other. If there were more accountability we would see less people falling in Christendom. There is rank and order in Heaven. There's also rank and order in the kingdom of darkness. The earth has established laws of gravity. There are laws of order to the universe and there is a God ordained order for the church where even the gatekeeper with the spirit of Christ is an honor. David said I'd rather be a doorkeeper in the house of God... It's worth His presence! (see Psalm 84:10)

In the book of Mark the eighth chapter Jesus encounters **The Centurion,** a man who is a great example of authority and submission. He had a sick servant that he wanted Jesus to heal. Jesus prepared to go to his house but the Centurion said 'you do not have to go to my house just speak the word.' He said I am a man of authority and I am a man under authority. I tell one to go and he goes. I tell another to come and he comes. He then told Jesus, just speak the word and my servant will be healed. Now that's a clear picture of true authority and submission. Neither is a one sided coin. The Bible says that Jesus marveled at the Centurions words and said 'Great is his faith'. By this story we are shown keys of faith, humility, submission and authority. We got to honor the anointing of God in leadership and we got to honor the Spirit of God in each other as members of Gods kingdom. If we honored each other more, there would be less bickering, more unity and teamwork. Gone are the days of the one man show. God never intended for His church to be a one man show anyway. Read the book of Acts, about the birthing of the church. There were 120 people in the upper room who were baptized in the power of the Holy Ghost on the day of Pentecost not just the leaders, the apostles. God wants the pews empowered so that as you go out into the workplace, your homes and your community, you will be as salt and light able to draw men and women to Christ. God wants more than just members. God wants disciples!

When you encounter people that desperately need help, you can't always tell them to wait seven days and I'll take you to church. You can't wait for your favorite prophet. They might be out of town. You can't wait for your prayer partner. They may be somewhere getting their hair done. God wants you to grow up and walk as a mature son who knows He can always depend on Jesus. He wants you empowered to pray for men and women at the time of need. As I said they might not be able to wait seven days on you to take them to church. Tomorrow is not promised. They could be dealing with a death and life issue. God wants us to be empowered witnesses walking in the authority of the Lord, submitted to Christ and submitted to the Christ in each other. The greatest among us must not exercise lordship over people but conduct themselves as a servant of all. It takes humility and death to self to do that.

> '…Jesus called them to him, and said unto them, Ye know that they which are accounted to rule over the Gentiles exercise lordship over them; and their great ones exercise authority upon them. **But so shall it not be among you:** but whosoever will be great among you, shall be your minister: And whosoever of you will be the chiefest, shall be servant of all. For even the Son of man came not to be ministered unto, but to minister, and to give his life a ransom for many. (Mark 10:42-45)

The need for unity in the church cannot be over stressed. The greatest, most gifted stuff in the body of Christ needs to go! God did not intend for his church to be a competitive environment of spiritual sibling rivalry many times spurned on by fear. The more secure a person is in God the less room for fear to operate. The Apostle Paul had to rebuke certain ones in the church for sin and contention. God said in Amos 3:7 'I do nothing without first revealing it to my prophets.'

Although this is a book on spiritual warfare and prayer, it is written from the voice of the prophet. God said to Ezekiel 'Son of man, I have made thee a watchman unto the house of Israel: therefore hear the word at my mouth, and give them warning from me.' (Eze. 3:17) There must be order in God's house from the pulpit to the door and part of the job of an intercessor is to pray for that order. The word of God says '… if they had stood in my counsel, and had caused my people to hear my words, then they should have turned them from their evil way, and from the evil of their doings'. (Jeremiah 23:22)

Yet, regardless of what is going on, intercessors must not usurp local authority whether you agree with it or not. For, the weapons of our warfare are not carnal but mighty through God to the pulling down of strongholds. Carnality—moves of the flesh in the pulpit and among the people in the pews is a job for warfare prayer! Your job in praying for the church is to do an assessment not gossip. You don't necessarily have to know all of the details but honesty for warfare praying is a must. Honesty is not optional in this war. Then God will enable you to develop strategies for praying so you can target the needs of the leadership and the local church body. Through authority and submission to Christ you can be confident when you pray that God hears you: 1st John 5:14-16 says:

> And this is the confidence that we have in him, that, if we ask any thing **according to his will**, he heareth us: And if we know that he hear us, whatsoever we ask, we know that we have the petitions that we desired of him. If any man see his brother sin a sin which is not unto death, he shall ask, and he shall give him life for them that sin not unto death. There is a sin unto death: I do not say that he shall pray for it.

You don't know whether a deed done was a sin unto death or not. Only God knows and can reveal that. So if God has not told you to stop praying and interceding for the cause, you got to keep on sending up timber. You got to keep on praying for unity in the church. You also got to pray for unity among the intercessors. For, one of Satan's main tools is to divide and conquer. The bible says 'For where envying and strife is, there is confusion and every evil work'. (James 3:16) 'But Oh how good and pleasant it is for bretheren to dwell in unity'. (Ps. 133:1) A house divided cannot stand. Neither can a heart divided. It's a house of cards doomed to come tumbling down if there is no intervention.

But how can you pray together if you can't even dwell together in unity? Prayer is an assignment from heaven. If we don't know it, we will find out sooner or later that heaven rules even in warfare. So we can't just pick and choose who we want. We can't maneuver to shut people out. Neither can we pretend the strife of warfare does not exist. Suppose a person is scattered and they were assigned to be there by God. The warfare of the church increases. Or suppose you as an individual gets sick and tired in the battle and just leave without God's permission. You increase your warfare.

The Ecclesiastic writer says there is a time and a season for all things. There is a time for war and there is a time for rest. You got to know which season you are really in. We have no business reclining at ease in Zion during war. That's how King David got into trouble with Bathsheba. He was reclining when it was the time and season that kings went out to war. (see 2nd Sam.11) So we got to work on our unity and we work on our unity by simultaneously allowing God to work on our love walk. How can you love God whom you can't see and hate your brother whom you see? We don't want to fight as one beating the air. The purpose is to hit the target—the bulls eye. (see 1 Cor. 9:26) Unity helps us to hit strategic targets and demolish demonic strongholds. Being on one accord helps us to win battles.

GODS AGENDA VERSUS MAN'S

Intercessors must not pray their own agenda. This is known as charismatic witchcraft. The agenda must be the mind and heart of God whoever hands out the assignment. Purity is a must for accurate discernment. We shouldn't call what's merely in our own minds, our own spirits, our own hearts the will of God. Many times we will have our own opinions. We got eyes and we can see. We got ears and we can hear. So we all can form opinions. We might be judging through battle-worn, weary eyes. So we must get our emotions out of the way so we don't pray amiss. (see James 4:3) We get our emotions out of the way through spending time with God in prayer. Listen carefully for the voice of God and pray according to His will. We have to pray according to the will of God no matter what we encounter. We have to execute God's desire even as brother Jehu did. The bible says:

> 'And the LORD said unto **Jehu**, Because thou hast done well in executing that which is right in mine eyes, and hast done unto the house of Ahab according to all that was in mine heart, thy children of the fourth generation shall sit on the throne of Israel.' (2 Kings 10:30)

Jehu executed God's will and did what was in God's heart. Much of what Gods will is can be found in the scriptures even for the local church and your own personal life. Then God also reveals His specific will in a situation. That's why you need to spend time with God in prayer so you can accurately discern. His will is backed up by the Bible. To stand in this war it takes morality and character and after you have done all you know to do, keep on standing. (see Eph. 6:13) You have the anointing to stand. You have the power to stand! Part of your ammunition is character, honesty, truth and integrity. So guard your heart for out of it the issues of life flow. (Prov. 4:23) If our hearts get muddy and twisted in emotions from enemy fire, so will our intercession get twisted or contaminated making for contaminated prayer! You end up with twisted lives—which is nothing more than a believer gone into captivity.

Let's take a further look at **'The Individual Taken in a Stronghold'** to get a clearer picture of how the church gets caught up in a stronghold. I mentioned the warfare of iniquity, carnality and flesh moves. These flesh moves can get you to do the wrong thing and cause you to end up in the wrong place, with the wrong attitude. Instead of repenting, you still continue to pray about (continuing in the wrong direction) as though God is going to change His mind. He already told you what direction to go in. Just because you want to go in another direction, His will has not changed. At this point the warfare intensifies because your will comes into direct conflict with God's will. God has a will. You have a will and the devil has a will too. We were created with free choice.

After we get saved, God does not take our ability to choose between good and evil. You had freedom of choice when you were a sinner and you can still exercise free will after you are born again. Therefore, if your will clashes with God's will the warfare intensifies. The higher up you go, the lower you go on your knees until God removes all the base things, the impurities, the dross out as gold is purified by fire. (see Mal. 3:2-3) The circumstances, situations and issues are part of the fire! The devil may show you some vile things but don't quit. Stay in the press. The devil is a defeated foe. He was defeated over 2000 years ago at Calvary.

It's a conflict going on and somebody's going to win. You can't give up and give in even if your own flesh wars against you. The word of God lets us know that the flesh wars against the spirit. But stay in the press. In the press you will agonize but you must submit to God like Jesus did in the Garden of Gethsemane. Declare 'not my will but Thy will be done!' God is on your side to strengthen you in battle to enable you to drink of the cup.

The Apostle Paul describes this war between the flesh and the spirit in Romans the 7th chapter and Galatians the 5th chapter. The carnal minded man is enmity with God and so are those flesh moves we make. (see 1 Co. 3:3) He is not talking about sinners. The Apostle is speaking to the church. Jesus said the spirit indeed is willing but the flesh is weak. Pray unless you enter into temptation. (Mk 14:38) That's why it's so important to pray. Your flesh is weak! The scripture says that the flesh profits nothing! So put no confidence in it!. You can't expect your flesh to help you. Your confidence must be in God and the finish work of Calvary! (see John 6:63, Php. 3:3) We are empowered to overcome by the Blood, by the Word and by His Spirit. In any given situation you got to know:

WHO AUTHORIZED YOU?

I was invited to a church to share my book on the subjects of infirmities, demons, devils and deliverance. The night before going I was in the Den and had fallen asleep when suddenly I woke up in pitch, black darkness. I looked toward the door and I'll never forget what I saw! That day is forever etched in my soul: *As I said I had fallen asleep but I distinctly remember thinking thoughts (as though I were awake) while I was sleep. At that point even though I was asleep it seemed as though suddenly I woke up.* So it felt real—whether asleep or awake I know not. Somewhat like the Apostle Paul when he said whether in the body or out, I know not. (See 2 Co. 12:2) This is what happened:

Suddenly, I woke up in pitch, black, darkness then I began to see small shadows of light coming in through the blinds. I looked toward the door and that's when I saw a tall, dark, foreboding presence come in. He or It came into the room. He walked over to me and pinned me down. This presence was powerful! Almost like God himself; except, that it was exceedingly wicked, dark, and pure evil. And it said something like this to me: 'You're trampling on my ground! Who gave you permission (authority) to go there? You got confidence? You got faith? You believe God?' And at that point, it was as though he hit me in my head (that is my mind—thoughts) and immediately my thoughts turned inward and began to travel backward. It was like a Spirit of Schizophrenia. I began to travel back in time, in my mind, in my thoughts. It felt as though I was traveling backwards in a bottomless pit or an endless tunnel. There was absolutely nothing I could do! Thought number ten became thought number nine, which became thought number eight, which became thought number seven and so on. It felt as though it was a never ending, bottomless, whirlwind-like pit!

After that I was awake and this time I knew I was awake for real. I tell you, I was terrified! Frightened and awfully scared! I was too scared to move but, too scared to continue lying there in the dark so quickly I got up and cut on the lights. The Lord then said to me:

> *'Tell Satan that he dwells in the thick darkness and there is no end to him because when God casts him into hell fire he's going to burn forever and ever!'*

As Apostle Daniels would say, Ho, Ho devil you got to go! I tell you the truth that morning Satan's attack was so strong that I literally did not wake up on my own accord. I have absolutely no memory of waking up. God himself delivered me and woke me up! As I love to say, God Did It! Later I learned that this type of hit has classification associated with spiritual schizophrenia. After this, Satanic encounter I did not want to go to the church but I went anyway as scheduled the next day and the drama continued to unfold. The first lady who had invited me to speak could not be found. The pastor was up speaking. I sat in the front. It seemed as though he did not know I was supposed to speak for even after his sermon he went on and on. I had informed her prior to coming that I had to leave early because of another obligation and time was getting far spent. I began wrestling with whether I should just get up and leave when finally the pastor introduced me and I got up to speak. It was then as I faced the people and spoke that I noticed the first lady sitting way in the back of the church. I thought that odd and kind of strange. I had felt the warfare throughout the entire service.

After church, I asked her why she sat so far back. She told me that she had been sick through the entire service and that was why. The atmosphere was shrouded in darkness. One of the deacons said to me in a strong sinister-like manner that was designed to do only one thing and that was to put fear in me: 'You think you're so holy but you're going to sin. You're going to sin if I have to reach in my pocket and pull out my own horns and see to it that you sin!'

There was more manifestation of satanic infestation but without revealing all, it is suffice to say that this church was caught up in heavy spiritual warfare. There was a lot of darkness manifesting including black magic and witchcraft in the pews. This is why Jesus said people should always pray and not faint. When people begin to faint iniquity increases (or vice versa) when iniquity increases people begin to faint developing strongholds in individual lives and therefore, in the church. Strongholds are developed and Satan can take an entire church into captivity. How else do you explain things like an entire church prejudice against another race of people? This church where I spoke at was taken captive!

That's one of the reasons why the attack the previous night was so strong. That's why the devil said who gave you permission to go there? It's my ground! The devil had gained a legal foothold through their refusal to submit to God. We always want to rebuke the devil but we forget that the scripture says draw near to God first. As I pondered Satan's claims to this church, I thought…that's deep! What does Satan mean? Does he mean he owns the pastor through some unrepentant sin and therefore lays claim to the church? Does he own the first lady? Does he own the rest of the leadership? Does he own some of the members? Is there a curse invoked by witchcraft? Or did they build the church on some type of burying ground and don't know it? The bible talks about the deep things of Satan. (see Rev. 2:24)

AVENGE ME OF MY ADVERSARY!

This was just a case example of corporate warfare to stress the dire need to continue in prayer and live holy, listen to God and walk in obedience. People don't want to believe in satanic entrapment especially after being born again but as with individuals, entire churches can be enslaved by Satan if they let him. If it happened in the Bible days, it can happen now. For, these are bible days. Jesus said continue ye in my word and then shall ye be my disciples. (John 8:31) It would be foolish to tell someone to continue in something if it were not possible for them to discontinue. This text puts a giant dent in the error of overemphasizing grace and forgetting the Father is a Judge and the Holy Spirit continues to convict when it comes to committing sin.

Why would the Holy Spirit convict you of sin so you can repent, come to God, just so you can keep on sinning? That doesn't make earthly sense let alone heavenly sense. There is a **Book** still being written in heaven which I talk more about in the last chapter. There is no new doctrine being written but it will help you to understand why I called these bible days too. But let's take a look at another example of spiritual warfare. I was getting ready to take a trip to Atlanta. I was going to stay in Lithonia while I was there. Just before I left, God illustrated corporate warfare that the body is engaged in through the following prophetic dream that I named:

THE FIRING RANGE

In the dream I saw many airplanes and helicopters. And they were coming straight at us! I was in a house but I knew that this would not help because as they flew towards us they were firing and shooting! These homes were large fine houses in a neighborhood to be envied to live in. Fortified brick homes! In the natural the communities looked so secure; yet, this would not help us. Neither did it help us. The warfare was awful as heavy artillery fire shot forth and so was the carnage!

This dream later manifested in several corporate attacks. That's why we cannot afford to take down from prayer and quit. You might get tired. You might get weary but the scripture admonishes us to be not weary in well doing. (see Gal. 6:9) Intercessory prayer is a part of that well doing. You're going to reap a harvest if you faint not. You need the strength of God as the battle rages on. Decree and declare: I am strong in the Lord and the power of his might! Perhaps some people suffer exhaustion, take down and quit because they feel like their prayers are not being answered. Perhaps some quit because they begin to believe lies, accusations or feel things will never change. But listen to what Jesus said in the parable of '**The Widow Woman and the Unjust Judge:**'

The widow woman came before an unjust judge who did not fear God nor regard any person. She wanted to be avenged of her adversary. The judge refused to hear the woman but she was persistent. She kept coming back. Finally he gave in to her and heard her case. Jesus said how much more shall God defend his elect which cry to him day and night? (see Luke 18) We are God's elect. So you got to be like that widow woman persistent. Keep on praying! Keep on knocking! Keep on asking! Keep on seeking! Keep on crying out until God hear your prayer! That word persistence means perseverance, tenacity, determination, diligence, doggedness, endurance and purpose. We want answers to our prayers but we got to be mature enough to allow a Sovereign God to answer. Some of us have not seen the fulfillment of the prophetic word we received because we will not help the church persevere through prayer. The church has a destiny just like an individual has a destiny. Part of our function in corporate prayer is to help pull in that destiny.

God spoke to me in another prophetic dream and said: '**ASK ME TO AVENGE YOU OF YOUR ADVERSARY!**' That's why the awareness of demons, devils, and deliverance is so important. We can't walk around here ignorant. Kids are dying! People are dying in sin and going to hell. Believers are getting caught up. Entire churches becoming snared! Yes it was finished at Calvary and the price was paid in full for our salvation. The devil didn't give up when you got saved though. The thief still wants to kill, steal and destroy.

We are still in the process of life on planet earth that the prince of the power of the air manipulates. That means war! We must be fully aware of demons and the need for deliverance. In the pages to follow we will discuss why the enemy has worked so diligently to remove belief in the devil's existence, demons, on-going sin and belief that there is a hell out of the church. We're going to see why the enemy has gone into overdrive to cheapen mercy and grace.

Demons, Devils and Need for Deliverance

3

WATERED-DOWN THEOLOGY IS HOT

People from all walks of life across cultural lines believe in Heaven. No matter what their denomination or religion is they believe in an afterlife, some form of life after death. Yet many churches and sects believe that there is no Hell. Some leaders hardly, if ever, speak on the subject though it's a part of their Bible. They teach that there are no such things as demons and devils. The devil is said to merely be a figment of the imagination from medieval times. They don't talk about sin either. I acknowledge that there are those who stress the wrath of God and hardly ever speak of the mercy and love of God if ever. Yet, many sects do the opposite and stress the love of Jesus and totally omit the judgment of God the Father that Jesus spoke of. (See Matt. 11:22) Some teach that the Holy Spirit only convicts of sin before a person initially gets saved. They teach backsliding was only in the Old Testament time. Many teach that Jesus was figuratively speaking whenever he taught. Some claim the Bible is merely literature, a book of metaphors that's not practically applicable for our lives today highly stressing and pointing out that men (who are human and subject to error) wrote the Bible. This is an attempt to devalue the Bible's authority. For a more comprehensive study that includes modern criticism and rationalism, I encourage you to get a copy of the book 'Lord is it Warfare?' by Kay Arthur.

Of course we know that men wrote the Bible but they were inspired by the Holy Ghost. (2 Tim. 3:16) We do well to take in account the context of scripture when reading the Bible, the time era and who they were speaking to at the time. But after you get through taking all that into consideration, you still come out with the Truth. Just like Heaven exist, Hell exists too and so do demons, devils and unclean spirits. People still need deliverance from these evil spirits.

There are some Theologians who want a bloodless religion with no mention of the sacrificial atonement of the blood of Jesus. I've even read reports of musicians threatened with losing their jobs if they dare sing about the blood.[2]

However, contrary to some modern day theology Hell does exist. Here are just a few of the scriptures that verify hell's existence: Mat. 5:22, 29; Mark 9:47, Luke 12:5. That's why we need to be in a Full Bible believing teaching church. Not one that treats the Bible like its myth, merely literature or some outdated source that is not practically applicable to our daily lives and so called modern times. Man might be modern with his technology but his heart is still old with treachery. Just listen to the news. The Bible says 'The heart is deceitful wicked above all things who can know it?' (Jeremiah 17:9)

Through Semantic manipulation it's possible for a person to make the Bible support anything they endorse just like a cleverly woven advertisement, agenda-minded reporter, or propaganda supporting show. Like a politician with a one-sided message, these false teachers have a gospel that is one-sided supporting their own lust. They will make a statement that is true and leave out the opposite statement that is equally true. They leave out the Old Testament and certain books of the New Testament. They leave out some text and only quote scriptures that tickle their fancy, placate their itching ears and support their cause. This method of manipulating God's word is old and from the father of liars himself the devil. He used the same method with Eve in the garden of Eden.

False teaching is a war on the Christ in Christianity. False teaching refutes the authority of the scriptures. But in regards to mans' refute of the truth and rejection of the Christ the following scripture is still applicable: *'And thou, Capernaum, which art exalted to heaven, shalt be thrust down to hell.' (Luke 10:15)* That is Capernaum, anybody or any nation that has taken on the spirit of Capernaum. There is a judgment day coming—a day of wrath, the judgment of the Lord. It shall be more tolerable for Tyre and Sidon at the judgment, than for the Lords adversaries. Obviously, Satan's domain has advanced in theological seminaries as the kingdom of darkness pushes to gain ground in individual lives, entities, churches and nations leaving the ominous question:

WHO HAS BEWITCHED YOU?

To believe false teaching and to teach false doctrine! False teaching is a result of spiritual ignorance, deception, witchcraft and all other satanic maneuvers. For example, a false teacher may say 'the book of Galatians is only for the Galatians.' But if you as a Christian whether you're a teacher, theologian or a lay person should find yourself in the same situation as the Galatians then the book is for you too. The scriptures say oh foolish Galatians who has bewitched you? Note this was after they got saved. This text proves that people can become bewitched and enslaved again by the crafty deceptive traps of the enemy and those flesh moves coming from the thoughts of a deceived heart. That is why when we pray we confess our sins known as well as unknown. We confess the sins of our fathers to ward off generational curses. 'There's only one good and that's the Father in heaven.' (see Mat. 19:17) In my book "Rivers of Waters" I talked about this New man with his old heart by examining the short story 'The Man From San Francisco' written by the Russian writer Ivan Bunin were he contrast the New world order with the Old world.

You may never come face to face with dramatic sensational encounters such as these described in this book. You may experience some greater. But no one is exempt from this warfare. We all have the enemy to contend with whether his tactics are overt or subtle. Through warfare in the mind, darkness tries to gain ground in our hearts and gradually our lives. But God showed me that judgment and hell are real through His Holy word and through prophetic dreams.

I recall when I was a young Christian attending a secular college. I planned to join this non-Christian club on campus. I thought about changing my life and becoming more politically active. I had been politically inclined in the past but was not actively involved. I had been born again in Miami. Sometime later, the enemy whispered to me that my salvation was an accident because the night it happened I didn't go to church with getting saved on my mind. In fact I went to the altar because the Preacher called me up there. But later, the enemy attempted to manipulate that and being a baby Christian I thought perhaps it was true. I was now attending school in North Florida when I had the thought that change would be refreshing. Well that night (since those were thoughts of backsliding) God had to teach me that hell was real and this is what God showed me in a dream that I named:

HELL IS HOT!

> *In the dream my deceased brother came to me and handed me a piece of paper as he said "Read!" I replied, 'I don't want to talk to you. You are dead!' Again, he said "Read!" Again I said 'I don't want to talk to you. You are dead!' He stressed in a urgent, forceful tone for the third time, "Read!" Again, I said the same thing 'I don't want to talk to you for you are dead!' He then said as he handed me the paper "Hell is Hot!" And suddenly I woke up from the dream terrified, in a state of alarm!*

The dream was surreal. Once I was awake and it dawned on me that I was only dreaming, I was relieved. I knew beyond a shadow of a doubt I dreamed this because of my plans. As I realized it was only a dream I thought to continue with my plans, since logically thinking it was only a nightmare. Right! Then the Lord spoke to me in a voice that thundered from heaven in my spirit: 'Repent! Or I will let him come in here for real!' This may sound ridiculous because the scripture says the dead know nothing. But don't forget God can do anything and I wasn't about to call a bluff! This experience reminds me of the metaphoric parable of '**Lazarus and the Rich Man**'. The rich man is nameless although the poor beggar has a name. I believe it's because his name is written down in heaven in the Lamb's book of Life.

> And there was a certain beggar named Lazarus, which was laid at the (rich man's) gate, full of sores, And in hell he lifted up his eyes, being in torments, and seeing Abraham afar off, and Lazarus in his bosom. And he cried and said, Father Abraham, have mercy on me, and send Lazarus, that he may dip the tip of his finger in water, and cool my tongue; for I am tormented in this flame. But Abraham said, Son, remember that thou in thy lifetime received thy good things, and likewise Lazarus evil things: but now he is comforted, and thou art tormented. (Luke 16:20-5)

What in hell do you want? Nothing I pray and neither do I. I repented of those plans! I changed my mind about joining that club and changing my life. 'What does it profit a man to gain the whole world and loose his own soul?' (Luke 9:25) Years later, during the early stages of the call, I was living with a roommate who was Catholic—a backslidden Catholic if they use such a term. The town I was in was approximately 99 percent Caucasian. I am not prejudice but I didn't know this prior to moving there. But I did begin to notice afterwards that everywhere I went people seemed to stare at me. Then one day at the grocery store, the clerk had the same stare. He offered me an application to fill out for a discount card. I really didn't want it but he insisted. I felt he just wanted to know where I lived. I also finally realized that I didn't see any black people anywhere that I went. So I felt that people were staring at me because of the color of my skin.

Well one day at the apartment as usual I was looking out of the window. It was the dead of winter and I absolutely hated the weather! Still my soul had to acknowledge how strikingly beautiful the scenery from my window was. Words can hardly describe the beauty. Indeed it was a winter wonderland. The winter had shut down the spring festivities. As I stood looking out the window at dead like trees with bare limbs adorning the sky, I felt like a stranger looking in. The bitter cold wind knocked my window out of the sill. I managed to get it closed and taped. I was out of medication and my body was being tossed to and fro as though it were by that same sinister-like wind blowing fiercely outside. My mind could not become content with either hot or cold for long before my body would shift gears again caused by severe hot flashes.

One night, I was awakened to the sound of voices of men and women. There was a card party taking place in the house that my roommate failed to inform me about. I managed to get back to sleep. The next morning when I woke up the place looked like the remains of a wild bar party littered by liquor bottles and cigarette butts. I was not pleased at all with this environment. A word of prophecy in due season was definitely needed and it came: *the stone that the builders rejected has become the cornerstone.* According to the scriptures you are either going to stumble upon that stone or be crushed by it. My living arrangements with my roommate did nothing but sorely vex me. In the struggle, these emotions were getting out of control and I had a warning dream of riding through the spiritual danger zone that I named:

ELEVATOR RIDE TO HELL!

In the dream death was a passenger in my car. Suddenly, I was in an elevator. I had a mind to go and see my cousin who was sick and dying from Aids. I thought he is probably going to die or is dead already so maybe there's no need to go. Even though the trip was expensive, I decided to go. The elevator had a button on the inside but no floor numbers. So I didn't know what to push neither did I know how the elevator would know what floor to stop on. So I just pushed a button, and down the elevator went and it did not stop. It kept going until it went down into Sheol! Pitch, black darkness and flaming red flickers of fire were all I saw surrounding the elevator shaft. I knew that I was in the heart of the earth. The darkness was eerie. The flames were so frightening that I closed my eyes and screamed! All I could hear was my screams! It was as though I was alive in a burning grave. Who could possibly hear me? I was afraid to open my eyes, for I would see the flames which were as though the Fire was Alive!!!

I had been on medicine for several years and I didn't want to continue taking pills. So for about four months I had been in the process of trying to come off of the medicine cold turkey. That alone would take me for an elevator ride or more like a roller coaster ride: waking up at night practically on the hour in a sweat! Then suddenly becoming extremely cold, followed by another sweat! Those severe hot flashes I mentioned. Depression was another symptom of being off of the medicine as well as violent headaches. One day it seemed as though it all came to a sudden halt as I crashed! The war had taken its' toll on me. We had been instructed to intensify consecration. Yet, it was a struggle and it's even harder when it seems everyone else is having a picnic. The lackadaisical, leisure, resort-like atmosphere did nothing but grievously buffet my mind. I may have been in paradise on the outside but inwardly it was turmoil. But the one thing it did give me was plenty of incentive to get on my face and pray and that was just what God wanted: Me on my face learning to travail, prevail and intercede in prayer.

A NEED FOR DELIVERANCE

Obviously there's no time to play church with watered down theology. God was teaching me and it was critical that I learn. I must admit it because this day and age that we are living in the devil's got pastor's seeing demons and committing suicide when no one's even chasing them. The warfare is serious! The warfare was real! I was asleep one night and turned over. As I turned over I became semi-awake when I perceived the enemy tampering with me in my sleep that is messing with my mind and whispering things in my ear, trying to plant thoughts. So I simply said 'I rebuke you Satan!' And I went back to sleep. It was after times like this that I began to plead the blood of Jesus over my ear gate, my mind and my dreams before going to sleep.

So, contrary to modern day theology, hell is real and so are demons, devils and the need for deliverance. Sinners need to be delivered and saved and sometimes Christians become ensnared again and need deliverance too. The Apostle Paul said do not become entangled again with a yoke of bondage. He would have no need to say that if it were not possible to become entangled again. Oppression from various forms, factions even in-house fighting hinders us from warring effectively. The Scripture says *No man that warreth entangleth himself with the affairs of this life; that he may please him who hath chosen him to be a soldier. (2 Tim. 2:4)*

One of the greatest weapons the enemy uses against the Faith is a spirit of doubt and unbelief. For example, after all the knowledge on hell I had, or should have had, God revealed to me that I did not believe in hell either. This knowledge dropped on me like a bombshell! Never mind God used Apostle Martin to deliver me over twenty years ago. Sometimes you have to awake a sleeping giant. You can read about the deliverance in 'Foundation for Success: Travailing, Prevailing and Intercessory Prayer' by Apostle Calvin Martin.

So God said to me '**YOU DON'T BELIEVE IN HELL**.' All of this was a part of teaching me and I was shocked! How can that be? I thought I believed that hell was real. Yet God said it and I knew it had to be true. But how can you be a Pentecostal, charismatic, fundamentalist, Bible toting, Bible thumping believer and not believe in hell? God said to me when you were a young girl. You read some literature by a very influential religious organization that taught that hell was not real and you believed it ever since. Then my eyes came open. The scales fell off like they did Eve in the Garden of Eden. And I knew deep down in my soul that I really did not believe in eternal hell fire. That was a lot to swallow and after the full knowledge and realization of the reality of hell fire where the worm don't die and the fire is never quenched, I wanted no one to go there not even my enemies.

This book was born out of part of that desire. Satan, the Accuser of the bretheren accuses us day and night before God. The devil also accuses God to us with such questions as: How can a loving God allow people to live in hell on earth and then send them to hell when they die? This is just one of the topics of hot theology. Read the headlines. It's taking preachers out! Some issues are deep. There are people walking around who are mad at God. They blame God for some tragedy, some loss that happened in their life. I was ministering to a young woman who told me she was mad at God. I was stunned because it was my first encounter with that spirit. That's why we can just gloss over people problems. Their problems are real. They are deep causing some to defect. Some take on new doctrine, doctrines of devils because of a spirit of offense. They are hurting inside and dealing with seducing, deceptive demonic spirits! (see 1 Tim. 4:1) They are struggling like a man in drowning water. Strongholds! I call it deep water and often quote the saying 'A river runs through it and its deep.' This war is serious and Satan is trying to take people out! One night, I was reminded of just how serious this spiritual war we are in as I watched the movie '**An American Story**' aired on PBS. We have no time to loose.

The story depicted how the battle heats up especially when you're sick and in pain whether that pain is physical, emotional, psychological, real or imagined. You can end up shell shocked! One of the soldiers mind was injured after returning from the battlefield but he kept on trying to live a normal life. He even ran for Mayor. Another one of the soldiers said I didn't ask for this. I understood completely. He was a wounded warrior. The soldiers said they thought fighting Hitler was a match until they returned home to their corrupt political town. This true story illustrates that individuals, churches and towns can become corrupt. The Bible shows us that even entire nations can become corrupt. Those are just the facts of war.

Yet no matter what is going on, no matter how corrupt things may seem, Satan is fighting a losing battle. We still have to pray and walk in a spirit of love. We have to forgive others and forgive ourselves too. I believe there is a hell and I still have my peace. We can love demons out of people. I read about a church who didn't know anything about spiritual warfare or demons but they loved Jesus and people. They loved the hell right out of people and God taught them about spiritual warfare as they went along. They were a sincere, humble people who walked in faith and integrity before God and men. They had a teachable spirit.[3]

Being spiritually shell shocked caused one minister I know to not only consider suicide but to attempt suicide. Suicide is demonically induced. If a person is wrestling with sin they do not have to believe the devil's badgering lies. We have an Advocate with the Father. *We must confess our sins for he is faithful and just to forgive us and cleanse us from all unrighteousness. (1 John 1:9)* Then we have to believe that we are forgiven. Tell the devil: *There is therefore now no condemnation to them which are in Christ Jesus, who walk not after the flesh, but after the Spirit. (Rom. 8:1)* Deliverance was needed and thank God for the minister who believed in deliverance and believed that that spirit could be cast out.

Another minister rashly judged them with harsh words for attempting suicide. But you can't be too quick to judge another person's dilemma harshly especially when you haven't worn their shoes. Some people are fighting dinosaur problems and others are swatting gnats. We have to judge righteous judgment. (See Mat 7:24) We are helpers to one another and that is why we must pray for one another. Some of us haven't been healed because we won't pray for one another. Look at what the scripture says in the book of James: *Confess your faults one to another, and pray one for another, that ye may be healed. The effectual fervent prayer of a righteous man availeth much. (James 5:16)*

We often quote the last part of that verse and not the first. But some of us are sick because of the way we treat one another. When people confess their faults, let us pray for them and make no mistake about it confessing faults is different from giving into the struggle and resigning over to them. The prayers of intercession need to be effective. We need to walk in righteousness and integrity as we proclaim that as Jehovah Tsidkenu God is our righteousness and righteousness has been imputed into us by the blood of the Lamb. So we boldly proclaim and let the devil know that we are the righteousness of God created in Christ Jesus for his workmanship. (See Jeremiah 23:5-6, Eph. 2:10)

God has given the body of Christ the five-fold ministry for the perfecting of the saints and our job is to point people to God. (see Eph. 4:11-13) The work of the ministry and the perfecting of his people involves deliverance and being brought into the full stature of the His Son Jesus Christ. The five-fold ministry is for this purpose. God does not want us to be overpowered and overcome in a struggle. God wants us delivered, made free and walking in victory. He wants us to put off being childish, grow up and become spiritually mature sons of God able to digest meat, never rising up in pride and forgetting that milk is still good for the body. (see Heb. 5:12)

CAN DEMONS BE IN CHILDREN?

Let's look at what the scriptures say about unclean spirits dwelling in children in Mark 7:25-30. This is the story of the **Greek Woman's Daughter.** This woman came to Jesus seeking a healing for her daughter who was possessed. The girl was about age twelve. This lets us know children can have unclean spirits in them too. The mother was a Gentile woman implying she does not know the ways of God but she was a wise woman. She came to Jesus seeking a healing for her daughter who was vexed with a demon. The answer he gave her looked like a deterrent. But everything is not what it looks like neither is everything what it sounds like. It's a good thing she didn't rebuke Jesus. This thing was ordained of God and because of her wise saying Jesus told her to go in peace her daughter was healed.

Proverbs 18:21 says 'Death and life are in the power of the tongue'. Proverbs 12:18 says 'The tongue of the wise is health.' That's why we have to watch what we say. Our tongue plays a part in the healing process. God help us! Take the coals and cleanse our lips! So we can speak with effective results words of life over situations and our children. If our children are unsaved or vexed with a demon they need deliverance too! The battle intensifies when the enemy wars against our children. Any mother knows this. You can end up in the spiritual emergency room, the ER of heaven hanging onto the horns of the altar for dear life. Thank God for a church that can serve as a spiritual ER room that's instrumental for spiritual recovery; for, in spiritual war, the battle can become lethal both spiritually and physically.

Another example involving unclean spirits in children is '**The father and his son**' who was tossed in the fire and the flood. The story is told in Mark 9: 17-27. The father brought his son to the disciples but they were unable to cast the devil out of the boy. When Jesus came on the scene the father appealed to Jesus. He told Jesus that the boy had been that way since his early youth. Jesus said bring the boy to me and Jesus cast the devil out of him. By these scriptures we also see that children can have demonic spirits in them. Adults can be vexed with demons from early childhood. Demons enter in at vulnerable moments and weak points in a person's life. Some babies are born addicted to drugs. All kinds of things can happen during childhood that open a door for demons to come in such as dysfunction in the home, sexual abuse, drugs, violence, emotional abuse, etc. Demons are out to kill, steal and destroy. They don't care what the age of the person is. They have a hatred for mankind.

THE SPIRIT OF THE JOKER

Once I was babysitting my grandkids. I was downstairs reading, studying and praying. My daughter came and got my granddaughter. My four year old grandson didn't realize his mother had left as he was upstairs in his bedroom. After they left, he came downstairs and asked 'where are my mother and my sister?' I replied, 'They are gone but they'll be back'. He seemed satisfied with the answer but then he kept on talking. I just let him talk while I tried to finish reading. Finally he said talk to me grandma, talk to me! He placed a demand on me. I thought, I guess I better put this book down and talk to him. I gave him the attention he so richly deserved and he was satisfied. Then he went back upstairs to play.

After a little while he came out of the bedroom again. This time he just stood at the top of the stairs. In a serious whisper-like tone as though he were telling me a secret, he said, 'grandma'. I answered what? He said, 'I'm going with 'the Joker!' I asked, 'you're going with who?' He said 'I'm going with 'the Joker!' I realized that he was talking about the evil, dark, sinister character of the Joker in Batman. That was the movie that he was watching in his bedroom. So I said, 'No you are not going with the Joker! You are going with Jesus!' He then said, 'I'm not going with Jesus! I am going with the Joker!' I shouted, 'No you are not! You're going with Jesus!' Again he said, no I'm not going with Jesus. I'm going with the Joker!

Then I began to do spiritual war on his behalf. I rebuked that spirit. I rebuked the transference of that dark, evil spirit behind the character of the Joker. I declared you are not going with the Joker. You are going with Jesus! After this confrontation, the devil quit. There was a dark force about to transfer and enter him at the vulnerable point of innocent childhood. He did not know what was going on. But because I had been spending time with the Lord he allowed that boy to walk out of that bedroom and tell on the devil. And God blocked it! When his mother came home she took that DVD out of his room. She spoke as though there had been a prior incident concerning the batman movie. I also knew about the actor who was playing the character of the Joker during the making of the movie. This actor committed suicide before the movie was finished. And I was like, oh no you foul demonic spirit, you can't have my grandson! The Bible says for this purpose the son of God was made manifest that he might destroy the works of the devil! That's deliverance which is also depicted by the following prophetic dream:

CAST THE DEVIL OUT!

I was in warfare in the dream and I was literally in a fist fight, fighting with a person who had demons in them when suddenly I heard a voice from heaven shout: you don't beat a demon out! You cast them out!

In the example from the book of Mark the ninth chapter, the demons tried to kill the boy. According to his father, often times the devil cast the boy into the fire and into the waters to destroy him. The fire and the water are representative of the works of darkness, drugs, addiction, violence, conduct disorder, sexual abuse, etc and the negative psychological and physical effects evil spirits leave. God wants unclean spirits cast out of people whether they are adults or children. But the disciples couldn't cast the demons out. Jesus called them 'backward' and he charged it to the whole generation by calling them a backward generation. They had gone backward from what they had learned and been given. This probably looked like 'The Big One!' They became doubtful and lacked the faith to get the job done.

When Jesus cast the demon out notice that Jesus told the 'dumb spirit' to enter the boy no more. This lets us know that after a demon has been cast out it is possible for it to come back at some point in time and will get in if there is an open door. Demons can come back with a vengeance! *'Then goeth he, and taketh with himself seven other spirits more wicked than himself, and they enter in and dwell there: and the last state of that man is worse than the first. Even so shall it be also unto this wicked generation'.* (Mat 12:45) Though this generation boasts of being modern, enlightened and sophisticated, they have gone backwards too! That's why more and more people and churches are justifying sin and evil because they couldn't get the demon out for one reason or another. They lost that battle so now they spiritualize it, agree with it and justify it before God and men. However that does not excuse their actions before God no more than it excused the disciples when they failed.

The disciples did not justify their failure and come up with new doctrine. When they were alone they asked Jesus: why couldn't we cast the demon out? Jesus told them that this kind come out by prayer and fasting. So when you are engaged in spiritual warfare praying, you need to know whether or not you are dealing with '**This Kind**'. Prayer is vitally important. For, deliverance is needed from outside forces as well as from within that is the 'enemy inner me" as Apostle William T. taught. Critical circumstances call for fasting and prayer. Such as when the nation of Judah was facing ruin and destruction, Hezekiah the King of Judah called on the prophet to pray!

HEART DIVIDED

In the book of II Kings, Hezekiah and Judah needed deliverance from Assyria. Judah had rebelled and would no longer pay taxes. So the Assyrian King came out to make war with them. Hezekiah appealed to the prophet and told the prophet to pray…**lift up thy prayer** for us… he said. God sent the message back that He would deliver them. (see 2 Kings 19) This was deliverance from war (outside forces) but we also need deliverance from within: In *Zechariah 13* God speaks of opening up a fountain to cleanse the people and to cleanse the land from sin and unclean spirits. In 2nd Corinthians 7:1 the Bible says: Having therefore these promises, dearly beloved, let us cleanse ourselves from all filthiness of the flesh and spirit, perfecting holiness in the fear of God. You got to fear God. The fear of God is being lost in the church. One good source on this subject is the book 'The Fear of Lord' by John Bevere. It's the church that Apostle Paul is talking to and telling them they need to be cleansed of unclean spirits. Filthiness of flesh is an unclean spirit of evil.

In *Judges 9:23* an evil spirit was sent between two people which cause one person to deal treacherously with the other person. In *Samuel 16* you read about an evil spirit troubling King Saul yet he still prophesied. In *2nd Chronicles 18:22* we read about a lying spirit in the mouth of the prophets which caused them to speak evil. One king in *2nd Chronicles 33:6* used enchantments, witchcraft and dealt with familiar spirits and wizards and caused his children to pass through the fire. That was a physical fire but we can still get involved in bad situations that can cause ourselves, our loved ones and everything under our authority to pass through the fire of trial and tribulation. Life has got enough trial in it without adding to it. We need to prioritize our trouble where we can.

Look at what God says in Lev. 17:7 *'And they shall no more offer their sacrifices unto devils, after whom they have gone a whoring...'* One of the kings was so evil he ordained priests for the high places. He ordained priests for the devils. *(see 2 Ch. 11:15)* Psalms 106:37 says *'Yea, they sacrificed their sons and their daughters unto devils...'* and people today are still sacrificing their children to devils through various methods including forms of media and entertainment. We were called on to do deliverance for a child who was being thrown on to concrete and against walls by a spirit. The child would break out in epileptic like fits while asleep, at school or anywhere. They never knew when it would happen and it was beginning to occur more often. We prayed for deliverance as we ministered unto the child and the mother. Thank God we got the report back that the child was okay and doing fine.

We also ministered deliverance to a person who was wrestling with demons. They were torn between two lovers as they found out trying to love two wasn't easy to do. They wanted to be free but those old demons didn't want to leave. Spirits were tormenting them in the mind causing them at times to do ungodly things. They wrestled a religious spirit and a controlling demon rooted in witchcraft and rebellion. The devil was trying to drive them insane. As we prayed for them, I rebuked the devil! I rebuked the spirit of insanity! I commanded the demon to go and commanded them to be still! They were delivered thank God and set free.

Once God spoke to me and told me to go to see a particular Mother in the church who was at home on a sickbed. God wanted me to warn her by what he had shown me in a vision. I didn't want to do it. I had reasoned if she was backslidden in heart it was a job for the pastor or some other high authority and not me. It was Sunday morning and I got ready and left headed in the opposite direction towards the church. The spirit of God took control of the wheel even though I remained the one driving and I turned. So instead of going to church I drove (or you could say spiritually speaking I was driven) to the Mother's house to warn her.

God had simply told me to tell her 'to clean up her mouth!' Remember the Bible says death and life are in the power of the tongue and the tongue of the wise is health. I couldn't add anything to what God gave me to say. I couldn't dress it up or take anything away. You can see why I didn't want to do that. First of all it would seem disrespectful for a younger woman to rebuke an elder. But I forgot the scripture that admonished Timothy to let no man despise his youth. (See 1st Tim. 4:12) So I entered her room where she lay bound by sickness upon her bed. I obeyed with as much respect as I knew how. I simply said God said for you to clean up your mouth! She began to spew scorn on me! Actually it was the unclean spirit speaking through her, trying to stop me. The scriptures say in Psalm 107:20 'He sent his word, and healed them, and delivered them from their destructions.' So I just continued to obey and kept right on speaking the word God sent me with. She scornfully said I was not (the one with the high title) but I kept right on talking. As I was belittled and called names, by the unclean spirit, I kept right on talking. I was accused of a demonic conspiracy and I kept on talking.

Finally I stopped and she had stopped also. I asked her could I pray with her and she said yes. So I prayed with her and she fell asleep. Then I got ready to leave as I was anxious to get to church. And she said in a gentle soft tone, 'don't leave. You are doing missionary work. I have been in pain and I haven't slept this peaceful in a long time even with medicine.' The peace of God had come upon her and in the room and I could feel it too. The Holy Ghost was the One who had been giving me what to say. So then I said the Word says 'to wear shoes that speed you on.' I knew that my work was done because the burden was discharged from my spirit as well. She spoke like Job and said though He slay me, yet will I trust Him. She wanted to know did God tell me whether she would get up off of that sick bed and I said 'I didn't know. He didn't tell me that'. 'It is the glory of God to conceal a thing: but the honour of kings is to search out a matter. (Prov. 25:2)

On another occasion we (the ministry team) were ministering and praying for deliverance, coming against the spirit of drug addiction. We seemed to encounter a spiritual barricade when suddenly the Spirit of the Lord revealed to me there was one on the team praying with us who had the same spirit in them that we were trying to cast out. They had a secret thing. They were addicted to drugs too. Of course this weakened the intercessory team, caused unnecessary warfare and struggle. That's why we need a clean house.

We got to be Holy. We were powerless like the disciples. Can you imagine Satan attempting to cast out Satan? (see Mat. 12:26)

We don't always know unless we get a word of knowledge, but God knows who needs deliverance. The scripture says *'The spirit of man is the candle of the LORD, searching all the inward parts of the belly'.* (Prov. 20:27) The Lord is purifying his people and his church. Where the altars of Baal have been erected, we need to tear them down and restore Gods altar. We need more purified intercession. Through intercessory prayer we join forces with God to defeat the works of the devil in our lives as well as others. Through prayer and worship we maintain a fortress in God sealed from the foundation of the world by the Blood, by the Word and by the Spirit which no devil or demonic force or hell can stand against.

THE STRONGHOLD OF GOD

4

THE POTTER'S HAND

Our central focus must remain on God despite the fallen condition of this world, and all the evil we see and hear about. We would be as men most miserable if all we discussed was the works of the devil and the condition of this world. (See 1 Co. 15:9) In all we do and say we have to see to it that Jesus Christ is lifted up. First, let me discuss why our central focus must be on Jesus at all times and at all cost especially in churches that believe in healing the sick and deliverance from evil spirits. Often the fire and warfare that comes against deliverance ministries is heated up seven-fold. The devil hates deliverance ministries. He hates the church. Satan holds people captive in his domain and he doesn't want them set free from the kingdom of darkness. Satan will fight a deliverance ministry tooth and nail. Yet, the church must maintain focus, its character, love and strong walk with God.

If not a deliverance church can get spooky and end up going on the wrong warpath, a path of witch hunts. People will begin to point fingers at each other proclaiming who is a devil and who is not. We must remember that we are in a spiritual war and people are not the enemy. The devil is the enemy and that is who the battle is against. God says let the wheat and the tares grow together. 'Let both grow together until the harvest: and in the time of harvest I will say to the reapers, Gather ye together first the tares, and bind them in bundles to burn them: but gather the wheat into my barn'. (Mat. 13:30)

Therefore, it is not our job to go around pointing fingers at people trying to figure out who is a witch, who is a warlock and who is not. It's God's job. If you end up trying to do His job, He's going to let you have a field day. You'll end up calling the believer a devil and making the unrighteous man a saint. For scripture says that which is esteemed highly among men is an abomination before God. That which is spirit is spirit and that which is flesh is flesh. If we are not discerning by the spirit of God for the purpose of ministering to the person by casting that demon out, then we are judging by a paranoid spirit of the flesh!

Often times we discern from what we see in the natural while God looks at the unseen and judges the heart. According to John 3:16: God sent his Son to die for this whole world. He saves witches, warlocks, the one you don't like and other notorious sinners too. God desires for none to be lost. Only God can say don't pray for a person anymore. We can't make this decision. We don't have a heaven or a hell to put anyone in. Things aren't all ways what they look like. The devil will throw a rock and hide his hand. By the time you look you see someone else. Or by the time you enquire about the matter and who did it, a lie is told and Satan's web has been spun.

Those who have belonged to Satan's convens have reported how witches and warlocks pray to Satan all night just to get power to break up pastors marriages. Satan dispatches witches and warlocks into churches to break up congregations.[4] That is why we cannot afford to fight and bicker with one another. These wolves in sheep clothing are known to shout like believers and speak in tongues but one thing they can't beat you doing and that's living right—that is walking in righteousness and living a holy life. So let God do the separating and let us stand strong against the negative effects of offence. As we watch and pray let us walk in love and forgiveness.

We will walk in love more as we cultivate a personal relationship with the Lord. If something is wrong with your love walk with your brothers and sisters then something is wrong with your love walk with God. We got to spend quality time with God in prayer because it is only in His strength that we can stand against the hot winds of persecution. It is only in by his Spirit that we can love our enemies as he has commanded and pray for those who despitefully use us.

God wants to meet with us. He wants to develop a personal relationship with each believer as well as a corporate one. In the book of Exodus the *LORD said unto Moses, Go unto the people, and sanctify them today and tomorrow, and let them wash their clothes...: And Moses... sanctified the people; and they washed their clothes.*

...And he said unto the people, Be ready against the third day: come not at your wives... ...And let the priests also, which come near to the LORD, sanctify themselves... (See Ex 19:10-23)

We are under a New Covenant but we still got to live sanctified lives. 2nd Timothy 2:21 says *If a man...purge himself... he shall be a vessel unto honour, sanctified...* We got to get in a quiet place and meet with God even as Moses brought the children of Israel out to meet with God. We got to wash our clothes. *...be washed, sanctified and justified... (see 1st Co. 6:11)* You need a clean house because 'A Clean House is a Strong house'.[5] God wants you to live a holy life. God is cleaning house individually and corporately. It's a purging, purifying and molding process whereby He is making us into the very image of His Son. He wants a bride without spot or wrinkle! We are the clay. He is the Potter. Jeremiah the prophet said:

> '*...I went down to the potter's house, and, he wrought a work on the wheels. And the vessel that he made of clay was **marred** in the hand of the potter: so he made it again another vessel, as seemed good to the potter to make it.*' *(Jer. 18:1-4)*

The enemy wants us to become marred and scarred from battle wounds in this warfare. He wants you to lose your temper and charge God foolishly like Job's wife suggested. The devil wants us to defect, give up, take down and give in so he can accuse us of spiritual adultery. The world says if you can't beat them join them and in the heat of the battle that is just what some believers and churches are doing. Paul speaking to the Galatians who had become marred and scarred said: *My little children, of whom I travail in birth again until Christ be formed in you, (see Gal. 4:19)*

No matter what it looks like or how rough it gets we are in the Potter's hand. He said no man can pluck you out of my hand! (John 10:28, 29) God can make us again as it seems good in His eyes not our own eyes. Think of what happens in a molding process. You're being crushed, hammered, squeezed, smashed, twisted and balled up! The scripture in Jeremiah goes on to say '*shall the clay say to the Potter, what is this that thou makest? Shall the ax boast against him who handles it'?* God is burning in our inner man the power and strength to stand. Through intercessory prayer God forges us and forms us into the very image of our Lord manifesting the ministry of reconciliation that God has given to every believer as priests before Him. (See 2 Cor. 5:18-19) Some of us go through more in the process than others for more reasons than one.

However, we got a ministry of reconciliation to portray to the world that is unadulterated. So we can't afford to let our love wax cold as iniquity abounds in this world. (See Matt. 24:12). Sometimes it seems like deliverance churches deal with a lot more iniquity. Though it seems that way they really don't. They don't deal with anymore iniquity than any other church does. It's just that the sin is more overt with more outward manifestations deviant from the acceptable norm such as drug addiction, drug selling, fornication, high percentage of one parent families, the negative effects of poverty, etc.

ACCEPTABLE OR COMPROMISED

However, I will say that acceptable norm has gotten wider and wider over the years. More evil has come out of the closet from the wealthiest to the lowest level of living in society. Yet, living holy is not optional. I am not merely being legalistic. For the word of God says, *'if we would judge ourselves, we should not be judged. But when we are judged, we are chastened of the Lord, that we should not be condemned with the world.* (1st Cor. 11:32-32) We got to develop this walk with God. It's like a marriage. In fact it is a marriage for God is not only married to the backslider, He is married to us too. (See Jer. 3:14, Is. 54: 5)

Therefore, our relationship is not a one-time thing, infrequent or only on holidays. You got to do more than just going to church that's comparable to a kiss. There must be intimacy. When you are married you don't engage in intercourse only once. It's an ongoing relationship that must be nourished and cultivated on a daily basis or the marriage is highly susceptible to disintegration and destruction. So we should judge ourselves by God's standards and search the scriptures to see if we walk in holiness, purity and faith.

We have to judge ourselves because this new modern man with his old heart of evil has white washed the gospel and drawn away men in their lust with itching ears to apostasy. (see 2 Tim, 4:3) The devil is using high profile people to push his agenda. Apostasy means "a defection or revolt." Apostasy is the formal disaffiliation from or abandonment or renunciation of a religion. But instead of renouncing Christianity these false teachers keep their organization under the umbrella of Christianity while they go about changing the laws to agree with their lust.(See Dan 7:25) This apostasy is comparable to the abomination of desolation spoken of as a sign of the end times. The devil is using the weapon of apostasy to attempt to redefine holiness and truth in the church and to make that which is unclean, clean.

The world is filled with natural toxins and with every generation it's becoming more and more toxic. It's becoming more filled with unclean spiritual toxins too. The woman with the issue was unclean. Mark 5:30 when she touched the hem of Jesus garment virtue went out from him to heal her. As we interact in this world, virtue goes out from us and we need to have it replenished. That's one of the reasons why you have problems in the church because of contamination. Antagonism is in the church. People will fight you! They only want to go half the way with God. They are living compromised lives and when they see you reaching out for more of God, they will come against you. Look at this excerpt from the book '**Antagonists in the Church**' by Kenneth C. Haugk:

> Hardcore antagonists are seriously disturbed individuals. They are psychotic...out of touch with reality...personality disorder...they carry a great deal of hostility coupled with overwhelming drive for power... You cannot and should not deal with antagonist solely on the basis of the good they might do. Only the historically blind would deny that Hitler helped Germany in some ways, playing a major part in a startling economic recovery from the pits of depression....
>
> C.S. Lewis said of antagonist that there are those who persistently say to God. 'My will be done and God reluctantly says in the end 'okay your will be done then... Offer your forgiveness with open eyes and a functioning memory... be cautious and don't be surprised by relapses of antagonist'

So don't be surprised by antagonism or by who the enemy will use against you. The devil will use anyone who lets him. But God is still in charge. He is a Father to the fatherless. He said *'if your mother forsake you then will I take you up.' (See Ps. 27:10)* The enemy can't keep you from coming into what God has ordained for you. We must use our spiritual authority. We can't let our authority be under-minded or taken from us. Every believer is called of God to walk in power and authority against the powers of darkness. The spirit of antagonism, the spirit of sabotage as well as other unclean spirits may war against God's purpose for your life but keep the fear of the Lord before you, not the fear of man. The fear of man is a trap! (Pro. 29:25) God has not called us to walk on spiritual eggshells. He wants us to serve him without fear: *...that we being delivered out of the hand of our enemies might serve him without fear, In holiness and righteousness...all the days of our life. (Luke 1:73-75)* We need the guidance and comfort of the Holy Ghost to keep our love from waxing cold in this vicious war. Speaking to the disciples Jesus said:

If ye love me, keep my commandments. And I will pray the Father, and he shall give you another Comforter, that he may abide with you forever; Even the Spirit of truth; whom the world cannot receive, because it seeth him not, neither knoweth him: but ye know him; for he dwelleth with you, and shall be in you. (John 14: 15-17)

FEAR WARS AGAINST FAITH!

Consider 'THE MAN WITH THE TALENTS' spoken of in the book of Matthew. The Bible says that the Lord gave to one man five talents. He gave to another man two talents and to another man one talent. The Lord came back to collect on his investment and the man with the five talents had gained and so did the man with two. But the man with one talent had not gained neither had he tried. Perhaps the man with one talent got snared by a jealous spirit because another had more. That's the wrong spirit. And the one with more shouldn't get puffed up in pride looking down on the one with less thinking he's superior. That's a wrong spirit too. God has given his gifts for trading purposes and advancement of the kingdom no matter how much He has endowed you with or what arena He has placed you in.

From outer appearance it looks like the man who had five talents and the man who had two talents had much more of an advantage than he who only had one talent. This judging by outer appearance is one of the most deceptive diabolical weapons that the devil uses. He uses this weapon to induce fear causing one to doubt through intellectual reasoning and comparison. This snare causes one to say what's the use? Thinking, the one with more talents has a much greater start. But we play with the hand we have been dealt. We war with what we have because what we really have is a priceless pearl.

The man with one talent let fear rule him and called the Lord a hard man. So Jesus commended the other two but rebuked and condemned the man with one talent. (see Matthew 25:24-30) If the man with one talent had only known that we have this treasure in earthen vessels and that God is able to do exceeding abundantly above all that we ask or think, according to the power that worketh in us, he would have done business with what he had been given and gained. (see 2 Co. 4:7, Eph. 3:20) Let me give you an example of the spirit of fear:

When I was in college, I was selected by my professor who was also a Priest to read my Final term paper before the class. This class was packed from wall to wall with students. I believe the title of the Class was 'Death and Dying.' One of the books we studied from was 'The Five Stages of Grief' by Kubler Ross. I didn't want to read my paper and I began murmuring. The class didn't have time for me to feel like reading my paper so they began murmuring. So I was propelled to get up and go to the podium and I began reading.

The title of the paper was '**Pages of the Book**.' I was nervous as I began reading when the Spirit of God spoke to me and asked: what are you nervous for? Look and see. You've got their attention. Their eyes are fastened on you. God opened my eyes at that moment and as I looked up, I could see they were captivated by what I had written. At that moment the spirit of fear fled from me as I finished reading in the anointing, power and strength that God had endowed me with from the foundation of the world. The fear was coming from what I had learned in my mother's womb, society, from culture indoctrination and man. To God be the Glory, the comments that followed from fellow classmates were quite rewarding and encouraging.

KNOW YOUR GOD!

So we see how the spirit of fear can take over in an attempt to cancel out the plan of God. We got to pick up and move forward though. We cannot afford to let the spirit of fear rule. Fear is from the devil and this world. Fear is not from God. God gave us power, love and a sound mind. (2 Tim. 1:7) Whoever or whatever is trying to cause you to walk in the spirit of fear is motivated by the devil. Rebuke that spirit of fear off of yourself! You got to know your God. The man with the one talent didn't know his Lord. He only knew what he had in his hand so he walked by sight. Sight walking is a grasshopper mentality. You got to rise up against it and say were not grasshoppers in our own sight! We're like Joshua and Caleb of a different spirit!

The stronghold of God is all about knowing your God, knowing who you are in God and knowing the authority you possess. You are a born again believer. You can't always wait for some man or some woman to tell you who you are in God. Your destiny is at risk. Get in God's stronghold and find out who you are in God. Cultivate that personal relationship. God uses men and women in our lives but he doesn't want them to take His place. He doesn't want us to make them God that's idolatry which causes warfare to accelerate.

Daniel 11:32 says ...*they that know their God shall be strong, and do exploits.* Another scripture says that *Men's hearts will fail them for fear, for the things which are coming on the earth...* (see Luke 21:26) So make up your mind which camp you are going to lodge in. You have a choice. The Bible says choose this day who you shall serve. Put off the spirit of fear. Rebuke it! Decree and declare I can do all things through Christ who strengthens me! (See Phil. 4:13)

I don't care what the devil brought to you whether it was fear or some other vice. Satan wants you to walk around ashamed that you didn't measure up so you can take down and give in. Repent! Confess it and rebuke the devil and move on. You got an Advocate with the

Father so use your spiritual weapons. The Bible says many are the afflictions of the righteous but God delivers him from them all. Declare: His strength is made perfect in weakness so when I am weak I am strong! (2nd Co. 12:9) Believe God for restoration. Believe God for your loved ones also because the devil fights us regarding them too. Speak words of life over yourself and over them too.

For in this spiritual war, you carry in your spiritual loins your unsaved loved ones. You carry them in your spiritual DNA. As we intercede for them, we must believe God for the spirit of salvation to be poured out upon our unsaved loved ones. God wants to save our entire household. (see Acts. 11:14) For the work of the church, our prayer is that God give us more intercessors. It's about bringing souls out of the camp of the enemy and into the kingdom. Jesus commanded us to pray to the Lord of the harvest for laborers. Many people want to labor but God is looking for certain kinds of people to labor in the harvest. This is what he told me in a prophetic dream which I named:

GOD IS LOOKING FOR HOLY MEN

In a dream I heard the voice of God say: God is not just looking for a man to preach the gospel. He is looking for a Holy man to preach the Gospel!

I belonged to a Holiness church when I was a new Christian. We barely wore make-up if any. Women could not wear pants and some of us wore dresses down to our ankles. I was astonished when God said to me one day: CLEAN UP THE INSIDE OF THE CUP! (see Mat. 23:25-26)

ABLE VERSUS WILLING

It used to be a time, when it was obvious, that there was a difference between a holy man and an unholy man. The enemy is working overtime to change that. But God not only wants holy men and women to preach, He also wants a people who will trust him and believe him for the promises that He has given us. Not only do you have to know your God is able, you got to know He is willing. The book of Mark contains the story of **The Leper** who said to Jesus, 'if thou art willing thy can make me whole.' There's a difference between able and willing. We must discern the difference so we don't waste time in intercessory prayer praying for our own will instead of the will of God. We need to know what God will do. (Mark 1:40)

I can just imagine the leper in the presence of Jesus. He has heard the reports of miracles. He sees everyone else around him being blessed and healed. Yet here he is in the presence of the Lord and he hasn't been made whole. He knows Jesus is able from observation and the reports. Yet he still suffers, with disease, despondency and decay leaving only one remaining question that looms in his mind: Is God willing? He doesn't waste precious time jealous the others are blessed. Instead of carnality, getting irate, mumbling and grumbling over his depressed condition the leper uses wisdom and says: Lord if you are willing you can make me whole.

Another example and case of 'Is God willing?' is when Peter tried to rebuke Jesus and block Him from going to the cross. But Jesus turned around and rebuked Peter and told him he was esteeming the things of men more than the things of God. That's high level warfare! That thing you're struggling with, does it look like the will of God? You got to be like Jesus when you are going through something that's pressing the very breath out of you. You got to know the will of God in that particular situation. Ask God 'is it for this purpose I was born?' Then you won't speak and pray amiss. You won't rebuke the devil when it's God at work. Jesus said in *Mark 3:34 if any man will come after me, let him deny himself, take up his cross and follow me...* Wisdom and discernment helps us to follow.

THE DICHOTOMY OF THE LION AND THE LAMB

I refer to the spirit of discernment as 'The dichotomy of the Lion and the Lamb—that is the Lion of Judah -vs- the Lamb led to the slaughter. You got to know the difference when you are caught up in a situation especially apostolic, prophetic people. For we get in that authoritative stance and start decreeing and declaring and rebuking everything. But you got to know when it is time to war like a Lion, decree and declare, bind and loose. Or is it time to be still and lie down like a Lamb led to the slaughter (give up the right for the wrong in a spirit of meekness) and know—for this purpose I was born—this pain, this struggle, this suffering or whatever it is. If you're not prayed up and walking in the spirit the flesh will cry out this hell!

This truth diffuses the prosperity gospel and puts a great dent in it. There has to be balance when preaching the gospel. For the word of God says: *'if you suffer with me you shall reign with me'. (2 Tim. 2:12)* There is a time of prosperity but we must know the difference. So we don't pray in vain or collapse when we're going through a test and everybody else around us looks blessed. Our prayers have to be strategic as we aim for the bull's eye. We have to be consistent in our speech speaking the word of faith and consistent in worship. We may have lost some battles but we win the war. As I slept on the sofa one night I began dreaming…

I had visions of various end time events… in my spirit I could see glimpses of the future and conquest for the saints of God.

God wants us to walk in faith. In daily living, if we don't guard our heart, we can get caught up in walking by sight. Joshua and Caleb were not confident they could win because of who they were but because of who GOD IS! The Bible says 'the just shall live by faith'. You got to be like the prophet Habakkuk no matter how bad it looks and declare: *'Although the fig tree don't blossom, neither fruit be in the vines; the labour of the olive fail, and the fields yield no meat; the flock be cut off from the fold, and there be no herd in the stalls: Yet I will rejoice in the LORD…* I shall climb my watch tower in prayer to see what he shall answer me. (see Habk 3:17-19, 2:1) To know your God and his purpose for your life stay in a position of intercessory prayer and keep your eyes steadfast on God!

The Lord talked with me in a dream one night about Satan transforming himself into an angel of light. Satan can do this in dreams, visions, day to day situations, etc. It looks identical but it is not the real thing. Instead of Issac, it's Ishmael. I called this dream 'In God we Trust versus the Opposer'. The devil opposes the truth. The Bible says that Satan will even fool the elect if God stay his hand. One of the major ways to guard against the deception of the devil is by guarding your heart for out of it the issues of life flow. Our weakest points are for things we desire, love or the things we don't want. When we got saved we did not stop being a human. Satan knows this so when he fails at one attempt, he will retreat into his demonic huddle and come again. But no matter how he counterattacks…

LET THE DEAD STAY BURIED!

There is a mystery regarding lawlessness and sin may abound but we do not loose heart. The warfare of iniquity has an end to it too. (see 2 Th. 2:7) I have a saying "if its' not stagnate then it's dead and everything dead needs to be buried." That goes for a stale situation, concept, individual or organization depicted by the following dream:

> *I stood alone at a distance looking and astonished by what I saw… I saw a woman dead as a door knob lying in a casket. I supposed it was a funeral for there were people around her. That woman was me. But I wasn't as dead as they thought. All was astonished when the woman got up. This is what I observed as I saw myself get up again.*

The devil said you're not ashamed to tell that. You're not going to tell that are you? But I am because it's too many falling down in Christendom. Ministers getting up out the casket and lay people too! But don't be alarmed by the dream of death. I've seen other people in caskets too and they went right on living. Death can also symbolize new life coming and Glory to God we all get up in the resurrection. However, this particular dream has two meanings. For one it's alright to get up when the devil thinks he got you down. We must know God not only for blessings though. For the scripture says to suffer with him is to reign with him. We want to also …know him, and the power of his resurrection, and the fellowship of his sufferings, being made conformable unto his death; (Php. 3:10) According to the scripture the flesh opposes this process.

That's the other concept of the dream. Our flesh, the old man desires to get up. Entire churches are being run off of doctrines of the flesh, which is nothing more than doctrines of devils. We got to put this flesh to death, die daily even as the Apostle Paul said. Jesus said except a kernel of wheat fall into the ground and die it remains alone. That is the death walk part of this new life, this new beginning. We died to the old man and all things have become new. Sometimes we apply this text to the initial salvation alone. And that's part of the reason many get puffed up in pride. Through their accomplishments, they think they have arrived. But I don't care if your following becomes the size of Hitler's! You haven't reached your final destination until they lay you out in a casket! Read the scriptures. The devil disputed for the body of Moses. (see Jude 1:9)

The Lord asked me one night in a dream: 'What is your joy in?' Before I could answer I heard a voice from heaven say '**THE JOY OF THE LORD IS YOUR STRENGTH!**' The python spirit seeks to overwhelm us in this war, swallow up our blessings and choke out our joy. We must overcome this world even as He overcame this world. So I commanded my soul to cheer up! I declared 'I know my Redeemer lives!' When he has tried me I shall come out as pure gold! We have to continually confess God's word over our lives. Isaiah 33:3 says call unto me and I will answer you. We call unto God in intercessory prayer regarding the issues and circumstances of life as we trust God to bring us into the perfection of love. Our focus is kept on Jesus as we are caught up in the stronghold of God's love, mercy and grace. The agape Love of God is a weapon. As we walk in that love and character we are strengthened to birth the promises of God.

TRAVAILING PRAYER IN SPIRITUAL WARFARE

5

THE SPIRITUAL BIRTHING ROOM

Intercessors-watchmen can be described as spiritual midwives. Spiritual midwives fastened as a sure nail in heavenly places. (see Isaiah 22:23) They are fastened in heavenly places, locked in to intercession, travailing in prayer to birth prophecy and the sure promises of God. Spiritual birthing bears similarities too natural childbirth. Inside the spiritual birthing room you travail in labor like a woman giving birth to a child. That word travail means groaning, agonizing, crying out, labor, hard work, breath blows and severe toil. Divine discontentment sets in until the burden is birthed. In prayer real travail concerns the energy we put into prayer, the force we put into it. We got to lock into travail and intercession.[6] When we lock into prayer we can stop the devils work!

There is timing in spiritual birthing. The number nine represents birthing. In natural child birth a woman carries a baby for nine months. The time in spiritual birthing can vary. It is based on the individual and what God is doing in their life. In natural childbearing some women when they get pregnant they experience what is called morning sickness. One of the reasons for this sickness is because they still eat for one person. They now have to change their diet and eat for two. It is the same in spiritual birthing. Spiritual morning sickness maybe accompanied by feeling burdened, depressed and weighted down. You've got to increase your spiritual intake. When God uses you to intercede on behalf of others and for birthing promises your time of intercession changes. Everything you do is increased. Your study in the word becomes more intense because you are now taking in spiritual nutrients enough for others. You will desire to be in fellowship more where the word of God is coming forth in truth, faith and power. Your desire to see souls birth into the kingdom will increase as God prepares you as a sanctuary for others to come and lodge in under your shade.

In the book of Galatians 4:19 the apostle Paul speaks of travailing in **birth again.** In natural childbirth you only birth once. Although, you may feel like you are birthing them again when they become older and begin to take you through some things. But thanks to God we don't have to birth them again in the natural. But in spiritual birthing like the apostle, you may end up travailing again for your sons, your daughters, for others and the church until we all come in to that unity of the faith. Here the apostle is travailing again in labor to birth forth mature sons of God.

The Apostle Paul said in 1ˢᵗ Corinthians 13:11 *'when I was a child, I spake as a child, I understood as a child, I thought as a child: but when I became a man, I put away childish things'*. So God is birthing forth mature sons. He wants us to put away childish things—the way we use to think about things and handle things. 'Let the mind which was in Christ Jesus be also in you'. He doesn't want us to walk around as immature sons with our feelings on our shoulders. He wants us to grow up. Free the pastor and the clergy up some for the spiritual babies who are coming into the church and for other work. We shouldn't be calling leadership every time we got a problem and definitely not for a headache. We must mature to the place where we can help others. In order to do this we need to get free.

A praying church is the place to come when you're having a problem whether it's with a loved one on drugs or some other issue. You shouldn't be ashamed to come to the prayer meeting and ask for prayer. However, some people are ashamed to come to the church and ask for prayers for more reasons than one. Yet, the world extends liberty to them with wide open arms to come to a bar and talk to a bartender. We're helpers to one another. We need to take the mask off. For, many times we get lost in a masquerade. During the midst of the services, title or no title, if you feel like crying—cry! If you feel like going to the altar for prayer then go.

When people in the church get free then those coming in won't have to deal with our drama. They can get free and remain free. God wants us empowered from the pulpit to the door. He even wants Holy ushers who can spiritually discern where to seat a person when they come in the door. Not merely judge by the outer man only and seat people on the front row simply because they look wealthy. The story was told about a wealthy man who disguised himself as a pauper and went to church. Despite what he looked like, he was still shown love from the doorstep to the pulpit and it made a profound impact on him. Not only was the church blessed significantly, they retained the blessing.[7] We need Holy Ghost filled Greeters and Ushers who can give a smile and a hug and someone gets delivered. You say what kind of hug is that? It's a Holy Ghost hug! It's a hug full of the love of God.

The scriptures say in Romans 8:22 the whole creation is moaning and groaning awaiting the adoption of the sons of God. Intercessors those spiritual midwives also moan and groan travailing in prayer for the maturation of the saints. When God is in the process of birthing you into a mature son, He is stretching out in you. Like a woman carrying a child she experiences stretching evident by stretch marks. There is a growing process going on and she is stretching. God spoke to me in a prophetic dream when I was teaching a class on Faith and said: I am stretching out in you! We end up with spiritual stretch marks from more ways than one. Like the Apostle Paul who said I bear the marks in my body of Christ Jesus. (See Gal. 6:17)

POWER OF THE THRESHING FLOOR

Prayer helps us to grow and makes room for God to stretch out in us. We stretch out in God as we lay out before God in intercessory prayer on the threshing floor. In the Old Testament time the threshing floor was used for animal sacrifices to God as recorded in 2nd Samuel:

> *'And Araunah said, Wherefore is my lord the king come to his servant? And David said, To buy the threshing floor of thee, to build an altar unto the LORD, that the plague may be stayed from the people...* (2 Samuel 24:21-22)

On the threshing floor the sacrifice was killed, bled and burnt. Today the threshing floor is the altar of the human heart where you lay and stretch out on the floor in prayer before God and you die to yourself. That is you die to your own selfish plans, your own orchestrated purposes and goals in life. Let God cut, bleed, kill and burn everything that is not like him—those negative attitudes, worldly mindsets and carnal habits of the flesh. We don't offer animal sacrifices anymore because of the atoning sacrifice of the blood of Jesus. Yet, prayer is a sacrifice as you spend time on the threshing floor on your face laboring in prayer and ministering before God. In travail you will birth the burden God has impregnated you with. Isaiah the prophet had a burden whereby he proclaimed: 'a grievous vision was declared unto him'. He describes the burden similar to that of a woman in labor:

> *Therefore are my loins filled with pain: pangs have taken hold upon me, as the pangs of a woman that travaileth: I was bowed down at the hearing of it; I was dismayed at the seeing of it. My heart panted, fearfulness affrighted me: the night of my pleasure hath he turned into fear unto me. ...For thus hath the Lord said unto me, Go, set a watchman, let him declare what he seeth. ...O my threshing, and the corn of my floor: that which I have heard of the LORD of hosts, the God of Israel, have I declared unto you. (Isaiah 21:3-10)*

We declare what we see as we spend time on the threshing floor. You need to see in order to birth the burden. Jeremiah the prophet said call for the wailing women, the women skillful at mourning and crying. (see Jer. 9:20) When you travail in prayer you could end up, moaning, wailing, and crying out to God for deliverance. This is not a time to be cute. People need to be delivered from some things and travailing in prayer helps. The moaning bench still works. It's not outdated. We can use creative methods to get people in the church but some things come by fasting and prayer especially a grievous burden.

The love of God and Holy Ghost power keeps them in the church. My son testified that one day he suddenly found himself struggling to breathe. He cried out for help the best he could in vain. Finally it dawned on him, he'd better call on Jesus for he was about to die. He called on Jesus and God delivered him. He couldn't call on his mama and no one else came. So he cried out to God for deliverance. The moaning bench is the altar at church or wherever a person finds them self in dire need. It's the altar of a heart that cries out to God in intercession until they get an answer to their prayer wherever they are. Here are some examples of intercession:

Eve, the mother of all the earth was a type of intercessor. She said, with God's help I have gotten a man child. (see Gen. 4) Eve was appointed another child the seed of the coming Christ. I also like to say after I have birthed a promise of God that I have gotten a man child. There have been times when I was just going about doing housework and the spirit of travail fell on me and I began to pray in the spirit. I liken it to the spirit of **Jael** who was just going about doing house work and God used her to kill Israel's enemy the king. (see Judges 4:21)

Abraham interceded for Sodom and Gomorrah that God would not destroy them if he found at least ten righteous men. (see Gen. 18) **Rebecca** the wife of Isaac at the time of her travail knew there was conflict going on in her womb. After enquiry of the Lord He told them that there were two nations in her womb. The younger would rule over the elder. (see Gen. 38:27) Here we see the nature of spiritual warfare going on even in the womb. When there is conflict going on somebody is going to win. You can't take down and give in. You're scheduled to win!

Hannah travailed in prayer to birth one of the greatest prophets known. Eli the priest came in and saw Hannah travailing at the altar. He saw her lips moving but heard no sound for she was in deep **anguish of soul** because she had no child and was being mocked and scoffed. She grieved in her soul. Eli thought her to be drunk but she wasn't. He communed with her and her request was granted and about that time next year she gave birth to a son. (see 1 Samuel 1)

Esther proclaimed a fast and called for all the people to fast and pray with her. In dire matters, sometimes there's a call for the entire church to fast and pray. On a personal level, it may be our whole household. Esther had to go before the king on an urgent matter were the stakes were high involving life and death—the very genocide of her people. She not only travailed in prayer she prevailed!

Jesus our High Priest, the Bishop of our soul is the Chief Intercessor who stands in the gap and advocates on behalf of his church. One particular season the Lord ushered me into a special personal and corporate assignment for prayer. God said I desire to see my church in intercessory prayer. His church should always have a distinct time set aside for prayer. This book is written just for that purpose.

The church is a type of intercessor in that we are God's *instrument* on this earth to reconcile men to God. The Apostle Peter was seized and taken to jail and the saints gave intercession without ceasing until he was delivered. Prior to this, James had been seized. The Bible does not mention a prayer vigil for James and he was killed. We can't afford to be at ease in Zion overcome by a slothful spirit. We shouldn't always try to throw away our trouble either. Trouble throws you into a discomfort zone where something has to give! Something has to change! You got to birth this baby or you will die trying.

Like Eve, with God's help you are going to have to get a man child. Like Hannah you may end up in deep anguish of soul. You may feel like you're all alone but you got to keep on pushing. Consider the rock you were cut from. Abraham was one when God called him. There are times when it may seem like people just don't care. If it's not them with a problem, they maybe slack to assemble for corporate prayer and travail for others. But if we were all up against the same vicious circumstance we would most certainly react different.

For example, when African Americans were subject to overt racism especially the Jim Crow rules in the south, people were able to get on one accord, come together, take action and prevail. Today many of them are now tremendously blessed in our rich nation. Thus the economic gap has widened the levels of lifestyle. People are not facing the same drastic, dire crisis and situation and Jim Crow rules as a whole anymore. Our personal situations dominate. Many times we feel like if we just had more money or more clout we would be alright. The worship of Mammon as well as humanism has gain more ground and even the church is chasing the American dream which is not the same as seeking the kingdom of God.

Yet the same devil still exists even as a whole. It's the same mechanism with different sophisticated maneuvers not only for African American people but all people and all nations. Satan is still at work trying to destroy whomever he can and any way he can. Many people are caught up and at ease in Zion. They don't treat the call to corporate prayer as vitally important to living a productive life. There's nothing new about this happening in a church. For instance, the church in Germany fell asleep while Hitler terrorized someone else's doorstep but it came back to haunt them all. We are our brother's keeper in this war whether we own up to it or not. Handling corporate prayer and treating another person's dilemma of less importance inevitable backfires increasing the warfare as a whole.

POSITIONED FOR BIRTHING

In this spiritual war, the nature of the battle can take a twist for the enemy is cunning and crafty. Just when you think you got him peg one way, he comes in another. One night, before I went to sleep, I remember quite well that I was in a very good mood. So I was well aware that I had gone to bed with happy thoughts. As they say 'feeling mighty happy and feeling mighty fine!' So I was in a good mood when I fell asleep. Somewhere in the night perhaps around 3am, I awaken for a brief moment and suddenly within. I heard myself say something negative like "I don't want to live. I want to die!" I was about to drift back off to sleep just as fast as I had awakened, when I heard an audible voice from heaven say with authority and power! "THAT'S NOT YOUR THOUGHT!" and then I fell back asleep. When I woke up I remembered what had happened and I knew why this happened. God showed me the level of spiritual warfare that I was in and how serious it was. God did not want me to become a casualty of war.

So the enemy can plant thoughts into your mind if you let him. Negative thoughts can create a negative attitude and desire. Desire can distract you from prayer, promise and purpose. That's why he does it to create a distraction, a diversion even a detour to get you off track. Initially you think it's your own thought but it's not. There are really only three voices: the voice of God, the voice of the enemy and your own voice. You got to know which one is talking to you at all times in this war.

Jesus said my sheep know my voice and a stranger they won't follow but you'll follow your own voice because you're familiar with it. If you get it crossed you'll end up short circuited like an electrical cross current aborting your promise. That's what the enemy desires. The devil seeks to short circuit your praise, your prayer and worship so he can abort the promise. The word of God is a two-edge sword so speak the word over yourself! That's what I did concerning that spirit of suicide the enemy attempted to plant in my mind. Like Joseph, I remembered my prophetic dream. I declared the word of God over my life and my situation. I said *I shall live and not die and declare the works of the Lord! (see Ps 118:17)*

Just like the devil attempted to plant the spirit of suicide in my thoughts, the devil will try to birth things in you too. He wants to be like God but in all he does it's evil, counterfeit and for his own glory. The devil tried to birth **'cancer'** into my body. I had just come back from taking a vacation. The hospital called me and told me that I should come in for my mammogram results. The technician said that they saw something on the x-rays with my right breast and they wanted to do another x-ray. Well I had another exam and I came back for the results. This time the technician looked at the x-rays and said she would be back. She took them to the radiologist and finally when she did come back she said that it was confirmed, they did see something on my left breast.

Then in a critical tone I said 'the first time you told me that you saw something on my right breast!' She sarcastically replied 'well I guess the other one wanted to catch up with the other one!' I began to rebuke Satan within. You don't always have to be loud. I said devil you are a liar! You don't see nothing! I was loud all the way home rebuking Satan, praising God and declaring His word: 'He bore my sicknesses upon a tree and by his stripes I am healed!' That was years ago and mammograms still attest that all is well.

The enemy will use various deceptive tactics to try and take us under and that is why the weapons of our warfare are so vitally important. We can use the weapons of our warfare to stop the devil from birthing his purpose. Our weapons of warfare are used for birthing our own God given purpose, the Logos promises which is the written word, Rhema words of prophecy and for birthing souls into the kingdom of God as well. We should use our weapons daily on a continual basis. The following weapons can be employed for birthing promise:

Praying in the Spirit is a weapon. Jude has one chapter and verse 20 says 'But ye, beloved, building up yourselves on your most holy faith, praying in the Holy Ghost, Keep yourselves in the love of God, looking for the mercy of our Lord Jesus Christ unto eternal life. (Jude 1:20-21) We often quote the first part and leave out the second part KEEP YOURSELVES IN THE LOVE OF GOD...

Davidic worship and the warfare dance is a weapon: (see Appendix B). The Bible says 'And David danced before the LORD with all his might; and David was girded with a linen ephod. So David and all the house of Israel brought up the ark of the LORD with shouting, and with the sound of the trumpet. (2 Samuel 6:14, 15)

'Let them praise his name in the dance: let them sing praises unto him with the timbrel and harp. For the LORD takes pleasure in his people: he will beautify the meek with salvation. Let the saints be joyful in glory: let them sing aloud upon their beds. Let the high praises of God be in their mouth, and a two-edged sword in their hand; (Ps. 149:3-6) (that sword is His word)

Worship is a weapon—adoration of God and who He is. The Psalms are full of worship. The scriptures say 'Give unto the LORD the glory due unto his name: bring an offering, and come before him: worship the LORD in the beauty of holiness.' (1 Chron. 16:29)

Despite the enemy's fire using the x-ray report, that's exactly what I did when I got back. I began to walk around my apartment seven times every morning and give God the glory and the praise. The storm didn't stop, it grew worse. Things got so bad, I didn't know what to do. The trial practically knocked the breath out of me and that's when the Spirit of the Lord said just Worship Me! That's when I became a Worshipping Warrior! You do war under the 'Dancing Hand of God' through prophetic warfare dance. Sometimes we think dancing is only for the secular world and the night clubs. But as we have seen with the Davidic worship, dancing did not start with the clubs. The Bible says in the beginning...God... We are rejoicing in the dance before God!

Sometimes we are persecuted for righteousness sake. Our time with God in prayer helps to keep bitter roots from springing up in the heart. Rejoice and leap in the dance for joy! The scripture says. They persecuted the prophets too. If you suffer for righteousness' sake, happy are ye: and be not afraid of their terror, neither be troubled; (1 Peter 3:14) The scriptures says in Luke 6:23 'Rejoice ye in that day, and leap for joy: for, behold, your reward is great in heaven: for in the like manner did their fathers unto the prophets.' '...the disciples began to rejoice and praise God with a loud voice for all the mighty works that they had seen;' (Luke 19:37)

Praise is a weapon and is not to be confused with worship. In worship you are in awe and adoration barely able to get words if you get any at all as your spirit is aware of how awesome God is. Hands are raised up or down on your face like the elders crying Holy! Holy! Holy! In praise you are usually louder, clapping your hands, shouting or dancing before God. David said I will bless the Lord at all times, His praise shall continually be in my mouth... God is not nervous when we are loud and neither is he turned off by silence. He said let all the earth be silent before me in Zechariah 2:13. The Spirit of God instructs us on what posture is appropriate at the time. (see Ps. 16:7)

Fasting is a weapon too. Remember in the ninth chapter of the book of Mark the disciples wanted to know why they could not cast the demon out of the boy. Jesus said this kind cometh out by fasting and prayer. Fasting reinforces your praying and strengthens your inner man especially during a time of trial and tribulation. Nehemiah and Ezra fasted and prayed regarding the ruin and sin of Jerusalem.

AVOIDING ABORTION

As the pressure mounts in spiritual warfare, it feels like artillery fire is coming from all four fronts: north, south, east and west. We want to be Frontline people but do we want to take Frontline fire? The devil comes to kill, steal and destroy. Satan seeks to kill the promise that God gave you. Satan sought to kill the promise holy nation of God as he moved Pharaoh to begin to massacre the Hebrew boys but Moses was saved to be their deliverer.

Satan will move in other individuals to get them to choke the word of God out of your life and to kill the promise. They are flesh moves satanically inspired to take you out of Destiny! That's why assembling for corporate prayer is important. In doing a corporate assessment we realize that (for the most part) our corporate house is as strong as our individual houses combined. We can't afford to leave one hoof behind.[8]

Maybe you say everything is fine with you. But we have to strengthen our weaker brothers and sisters because everybody is not as spiritually strong and prayed up. You may be doing well in your prayer closet at home. But your spiritual praying is still needed in church to help those who are weaker and to help birth the destiny of the ministry. The Bible speaks of being stuck in the birth canal with no strength to bring forth. (see Is. 37:3) We don't want to be stuck in the birth canal in warfare… dreams stuck, hopes stuck, ministry stuck, etc. So no matter who the enemy uses you don't have to be stuck in the birth canal.

You can birth your own promise even if it is intricately woven with others involved. Remember the rock you were cut from. Abraham was one when God called him. We don't want to get stuck in spiritual time warps…demonic cycling; blind sighted by issues and circumstances. Thereby reinforcing fear rather than maintaining focus on God who strengthens our faith. Distractions, diversions and detours can cause you to become stuck looking for a healing but never receiving one. The Bible says in Deuteronomy 32:39 *they looked for a healing but only a continual stroke came*. Why was that so? They were stuck in demonic cycling. Always saying it's a new beginning but using the same old dead methods that got them stuck in the first place. It is said that it is insanity to do the same thing and expect different results. God said in second Chronicles:

> '*If I shut up heaven that there be no rain, or if I command the locusts to devour the land, or if I send pestilence among my people; If my people, which are called by my name, shall humble themselves, and pray, and seek my face, and turn from their wicked ways; then will I hear from heaven, and will forgive their sin, and will heal their land...* (2 Chron. 7:12-16)

In Isaiah 66:9 God said *'Shall I bring to birth and not deliver?'* But some labor is hard labor. Ask a woman. You're not going to bring this baby forth as easy as the others. This assignment on your life is bigger this time around. God is stretching out in you. Therefore carrying this baby and the birthing of it is harder. Just like God revealed to Rebecca the conflict and intensity of what was going on in her womb, when I was going through a very difficult time the Lord showed me what it meant in a dream that I named:

HARD LABOR

I was lying down practically naked on my side in labor (the labor may have been in my mind) but nevertheless I was in labor and it was hard labor, very difficult and I pushed and pushed! Then I turned over on my back and my legs were spread. One part of the window had no curtains and I feared being seen. Then I was completely naked and exposed and maybe even outside.... Just before I woke up, I heard **'In the beginning** *God created the heaven and the earth and the earth was without form and darkness was upon the face of the deep and the Spirit of God was hovering over it...'*

You certainly don't birth lying on your side. And you lose all worry as to whose looking at you when you are having labor pain. The spirit of Tobiah and Sanballat (mocker and scoffer) gets louder when your nakedness is exposed. But God said all things are naked and open to Him. (See Heb. 4:13) The voice of the Lord that I heard depicts what is happening in the spirit realm during the birthing process. God is making something new despite all the chaos, darkness and mess going on in spiritual warfare. Remember the assignment of the intercessor is two-fold, personally and corporately. This makes the birthing more difficult because it's like carrying twins in the spirit realm. Labor is hard and in the natural some labor is so hard the woman can't birth for different reasons and she ends up having a C-section a caesarean birth. You can die in childbirth that's why we need to be like Eve and know with God's help I'll get a man child.

Years ago when I was carrying my oldest child, I remember crying thinking he wasn't ever going to come. He was overdue. That will happen sometimes inside the waiting room. You start saying things like how long God? God may look at you and ask how long? How long must I bear with you 'you untoward generation?' (see Mark 9:19) But my oldest child was a big baby. I ended up having hard labor. They had to take him! He seemed to take forever to come and now that he was coming, I was unable to deliver him. Women are unable to deliver for different reasons so the baby has to be taken. All truth is parallel—as in natural childbirth so in spiritual birthing. Sometimes the spiritual baby has to be taken too by someone else. The one carrying for various reasons is unable to deliver them.

WHICH IS EASIER?

Contrary to some faith teaching, there are just some things you just can't do. Some things are extremely difficult. If they walked away from Jesus, they will walk away from you. Mark the 10th chapter tells the story of '**The Rich Young Ruler**' Jesus told the rich young ruler to sell all he had and come and follow him. The young ruler didn't want to do it. So he went away sad because he had great substance. Jesus then said how hard it is for a rich man to enter the kingdom. The disciples said who then can be saved? You see the desperation and the impossibility even of salvation and we're not even speaking of healing or casting the devil out at this point. However, Jesus said with men it may be impossible but with God, all things are possible. Do you think Jesus would have said this if it were not true? Some things you just can't do. Don't let people bring you into bondage by criticizing you saying you just don't have enough faith. That may be true at times but not at all times.

Mark the 2nd chapter we find the story of 'THE PARALYTIC MAN' who was carried by four on the stretcher. They broke up the roof and let the man down right in front of Jesus. The Bible says Jesus saw their faith. Jesus said unto him thy sins be forgiven thee. Those present began to murmur and say who can forgive sins besides God? But Jesus answered them and said which is easier? To say thy sins are forgiven thee or rise up, take up thy bed and walk. We know some natural things are harder such as mountain climbing. If it wasn't harder everybody would be doing it. But we can also see by this saying that some spiritual things are harder than others. Hard things involve harder labor whereby it takes travailing, prevailing and interceding in prayer even more so. Years can go into a particular assignment. Some assignments are like nurturing after birthing. Nurturing is another part of the process it just takes longer. The going is not always easy whether birthing or nurturing. Some birth but for various reasons are unable to nurture. It takes much more commitment and love to nurture in this war.

God is still a part of the process though. He is the Grand weaver. Nurturing takes longer and so do some spiritual assignments. We must hold the fort longer through all the artillery fire. Our love and commitment will be tried by fire sevenfold because we're holding the position longer. We must continue to use our weapons. Despite the hot winds of persecution and hate that we receive in this world, we must continue to walk in the agape love of God, continue to worship, and continue to pray. For Jesus said *'ye shall be hated of all men for my name's sake: He that endureth to the end, the same shall be saved.* (Matt. 10:22) So let us be minded like the four men that carried the paralytic man, breakup the fallow ground that's trying to hold us back from the manifestation of the prophetic word. Let God see our faith too as we press on to prevail in prayer for our miracle, our Destiny!

PREVAILING PRAYER
IN SPIRITUAL WARFARE

6

WARFARE PRAYING!

We are an end-time Joshua like generation. We are warriors in the spirit. In spiritual warfare prayer, prevailing prayer is that prayer that gets the victory. That word prevail means to overcome, to conquer, to win. In Prevailing prayer you don't talk defeat! In Prevailing prayer you don't think defeat! You only think the victory!

Though we live in a fallen world no matter how many times negative forces come against us, we must continue to resist negative thoughts of defeat, discouragement, doubt and unbelief. The scripture says in James 4:7 '…submit yourself to God first, resist the devil and he will flee! We must put our 'all' on the altar and declare I can do all things through Christ Jesus who strengthens me! (see 1 Cor. 2:16, Phil. 4:13)

We have to stand strong against oppositional forces of offense. You might ask how often? In the grammar school I attended, if you got into trouble the teacher would make you write sentences five-hundred times stating: 'I will not get into trouble.' Well trouble knocked and I ended up having to write those sentences 500 times. I couldn't stop until it was done or it was a trip to the principal's office.

The disciple asked Jesus: how often shall I forgive my brother seven times? You see they already had a time frame established in their mind, but Jesus said no I say seventy-seven times seven. There is a timing of God in all situations that we encounter. In the love of Christ Jesus, we must do what has to be done in order to get the assignment done.

Persevere! God would not tell us to forgive someone 77 x 7 and then not forgive us because we fell short of the mark. We wage a good warfare as we stay in the press toward the mark for the prize of the high calling. (see Phil. 3:14) If we fall we get back up. We confess it, repent and receive by faith forgiveness. All that we do for God is in Christ Jesus even our warfare. We're not fighting the devil. We fight the good fight of faith! (1 Tim. 6:12)

There must be a paradigm shift in our mindset. We need more than a well-made up mind. We need the mind of Christ! A well made up mind will only get you so far when the fire of persecution and suffering come. We must allow the old way of thinking to die and be renewed. How? By the transforming of your mind! The Bible says in Psalm 1:1 'Blessed is the man that walks not in the counsel of the ungodly…' The mind of the old man is ungodly therefore we should not listen to it.

We engage in a level of high spiritual warfare as we prevail in prayer. Things are shaken up in warfare. God said once more I will again 'Shake the heavens and the earth.' (Heb. 12:26, Hag. 2:6) But God always has a remnant and He will use what remains. (Zech. 8:12) We may begin to feel shaken up due to all the warfare but we can't afford to get tangled up into confusion. Shake it off like Paul shook off the viper. (See Acts 28:3) Shake it off through the power of prevailing prayer, by the blood, by the word and the Spirit!

Jesus said behold I give you power to tread on serpents and scorpions over all the forces of the enemy and nothing by any means shall harm you. (Luke 10:19) God is in control even in the midst of heavy warfare! God took the prophet Ezekiel behind the wall to see what the people were doing. Sometimes God will allow you to see what's going on. But don't faint because of the evil you see and hear about in this world. Pray! Otherwise you could end up taking a direct hit. Frontline warfare and heavy artillery fire are illustrated in the following dream:

BLACK BIRDS FLY BY THE LIGHT OF THE MOON
In the dream, I had a conversation with a sister who had left the church. She was telling me why she left and how she felt she had too. In another dream or perhaps the same one I was in a vehicle with the intercessors. Witches represented by black birds were flying in the sky above us. One of the intercessors pointed them out. Then suddenly there were black jet fighting aircrafts flying above! So many that they

> *backed up in air traffic! The traffic even backed up on the ground.* (This traffic jam represented heavy warfare, witches, warlocks and the powers of darkness) *I said to the intercessor that pointed to the birds, let's cut across that field to get out of the direct path of them. As we cut across, we had to push and help propel our vehicle with our feet.*

Several manifestations of undercover evil as well as overt works of the devil took place. For example, I was looking out of the window on the job one day. I'm a lover of nature. From my earliest childhood I have always stared out the window in admiration, mesmerized by the beauty of the trees, the earth and the sky. This particular day, I was very concerned about someone I had been interceding for. They were caught up in heavy artillery fire. When iniquity increases so do the manifestations of warfare. As I looked out of the window I saw two large blackbirds fly by into the tree right by where my car was parked in the parking lot. I marveled at the huge size of them. Then as I stood looking, one bird flew right in front of the window faced me and did some kind of technique... I really don't know what to call it, like a flying dance, a flying trapeze maneuver or a flying airshow display... It was as though the bird mocked me! Then he perched in the tree near the window... The voice of the mocker, naysayer and gainsayer gets worse as the battle heats up. The enemy will whisper things like praying is not going to help...things will never change. He wants us to say what's the use? He wants us to become discouraged and take down. He'll put satanic stumbling blocks in the way. The enemy is not just going to sit by idly and watch you prevail in prayer. So he uses his agents: the spirit of the mocker, the scoffer which is the spirit of Tobiah, Sanballat and Gershom who scoffed at Nehemiah and tried to block them from rebuilding the ruins of Jerusalem.

At another time, I was at home sitting in the living room looking out of the window at the bare trees with grey, ghost limb-like fingers spread out etching the blue skyline when suddenly a host of blackbirds flew in and perched on the branches. I tell you it looked like a thousand birds. They evidently didn't get the memo, that it was winter now and the birds had flown south. They faced the east toward my window. I thought about their representation of the high level witchcraft, occult activity and warfare going on. I must say it was a day of hell with much contention in it.

The next day as I looked out of the window they flew back again and perched in the bare, grey, ghost-like looking branches. But this time I was fed up and I said not today devil! I rose up in spiritual authority and began to rebuke the Jezebel spirit, the spirit of witchcraft, evil spirits, wicked rulers, hostility, marine spirits, water sprits, etc. Within an hour they all flew away. During this stage of my life, there was a lot of animal manifestation representing the demonic activity going on. One night we were in prayer and towards the end of the prayer a bat manifested and flew straight through the middle of us. 'A bat represents a night dweller, thought to suck blood—unclean flying creature often related to witchcraft and vampires'. (See Duet. 14:18, Is. 2: 19-21, Lev. 11:19. Internet source: From Joshua Media Ministries)

This reminds me of a story I was told about a church whose pastor didn't like minorities. He told his members if blacks come to the church treat them nice but don't invite them back. He was in his 40's or early 50's and not long after, he died and the church broke up. Later the property was bought by a black pastor. When they went to the church they could hardly get in the doors for all the blackbirds that were in the area. It was like the movie 'The Birds' there were so many. So they ended up having to do spiritual warfare praying in that church sometimes spending whole nights in ward praying, pleading the blood of Jesus throughout the sanctuary. By the time they got to the last area they were at the church door and all those birds had left. Heavy witchcraft and warfare had gone on against that church. We must do more in corporate prayer. We got to do intensive, effectual prayer.

This event brings to my mind the time I was sitting in a church service listening to a pastor preach when suddenly right in the middle of his sermon he said 'white people are blue-eyed devils.' I was like oh my God! Enemy spotted! Tares mixed with wheat! That minister obviously needed deliverance because racism is not of God! God is love and not hate. He was contaminated! Spiritually toxic! I don't know what he had been through or what his warfare had been like but it caused contamination in the heart.

Another animal manifestation took place while I was in my living room. The night before, I had had a fitful night's sleep. I got up early and went into prayer. I was praying out loud when a squirrel made a loud squeaking, screeching sound with his paws across the window as he stretched his body long across the pane. I was grossly irritated. I had seen more squirrels the short time that I lived there than I had seen in all my years of living. I had even seen squirrels on my balcony rail with food, even pizza in their mouth staring at me. I couldn't stand those squirrels! I would close the shades, which is not a solution for a nature lover because then I felt closed in. This type of activity would go on all day sometimes.

Many times the squirrels tumbled making rumbling sounds as though they fought a war with each other on the roof right above my head. Although, I noticed this didn't occur while I was praying. But then one day things got so bad until they began tumbling and rumbling as I was praying right above my head on the roof. This symbolized a severe level of warfare. I rebuked Satan's activity using animals to buffet me. The weather was coming in strong and relentless. It was a severe winter. Pouring down like torrential rains, it was one storm right after the other, snowing hard like the heavens themselves were at war!

WARFARE & SPIRITUAL VIOLENCE

The enemy manifests in different manners in warfare. Just when you think you got his methods pinned down one way, he comes in another. Many times we do not see the spiritual side. We only see the manifestation of the natural. These manifestations can take place in our lives anywhere in the community. You're having problems at home and don't understand why. Warfare! You're having a problem on the job and don't understand why. Warfare! You're having problems in church and don't understand why. Warfare! The kingdom of heaven suffereth violence, and the violent take it by force. (Mat 11:12) I worked at a facility that had some maximum lockdown classification. War was going on between the staff as well as with others. Things got so bad it manifested. I thought I was going to work but I was destined to find out just what I was really going to. I began to have warfare dreams. The first prophetic dream I named:

NOT WORK BUT A PRAYER MEETING

I was dreaming but it was so real that I actually thought that I had gone to work. But where I went did not look like my job. A lady (leader, manger) was up front and another lady that had the look (disposition) of my supervisor was there and she pulled a knife out to cut the leader. So in the dream I remember thinking: I thought I was going to work but I was going to a prayer meeting. Here is the other dream that I named:

EVIL MANIFESTED

In the dream I was lying in the bed when something evil began coming up from the side of the bed. A evil hand emerged from the side of the bed right beside me...it felt as though a hand from the cemetery reached up. At first I was afraid but then I reached out my hand and grasped the evil hand in defiance to defeat it and the evil presence lessened. But as I warred with it, the evil began to manifest from another part of the bed near my head...

These dreams symbolized the warfare taking place on the job and off. There were real threats of bodily harm made by staff members including leaders against each other. Lawsuits broke out! At God's request, other than my normal prayers, I had done spiritual warfare prayer on the job when I was alone: anointing the area, doing warfare prayer, binding and loosing, decreeing and declaring what was going to be and what was not going to be tolerated to the point things began to change. The leadership took notice and began to commend my work but the devil didn't like this. As Pastor L.C. Callahan used to say 'The devil don't like this! The devil don't like this! The devil don't like this!'

So the enemy launched a counter attack. Unbeknown to me a threat was made against my life on the job. I found out about 9pm that night. The threat had been made that morning to kill me! It seems everyone had known including the police who were called in except me until that night. They were concerned for my life but I wasn't afraid. Things got really wild and crazy. One comment made by the one who threatened me was 'that I wouldn't stop playing Christian music.' When this was said the supervisor said 'I want a copy of that CD!' Well it is suffice to say that God blocked it! They wanted me to help prosecute the person but I wouldn't. This particular manifestation of the warfare was represented by the dream 'Evil manifested'. The one that threatened to kill me had previously boasted on the job that their father was a king and a warlock in a foreign country that was heavy in voodoo practices. The devil was mad because through prevailing warfare prayer, I had gone into his domain and began to sabotage it taking souls for the kingdom of God.

For effective warfare, when it comes to warring for your prophesy warring for your destiny, and warring for souls, you got to assess everything in your life and every person including your own spirit. You got to know who your friends are and who's not. What I mean is you got to know what spirit they are coming in when they approach your space. It could be a relative a close relative. It doesn't matter. The Bible says in the book of Joshua:

> *And it came to pass, when Joshua was by Jericho, that he lifted up his eyes and looked, and, behold, there stood a man over against him with his sword drawn in his hand: and Joshua went unto him, and said unto him, Art thou for us, or for our adversaries? And he said, Nay; but as captain of the host of the LORD am I now come. And Joshua fell on his face to the earth, and did worship, and said unto him, What saith my lord unto his servant? (Joshua 5:13-14)*

When assessing a situation we also got to ask the question **'FRIEND OR FOE?'** If they are a foe, deal with it like that including your own spirit. The scripture says the flesh wars against the spirit. Jesus said the flesh profits nothing! It's the spirit that quickeneth. (See John 6:63) Love people, continue to pray for them but feed them with a long handle spiritual spoon. Some of you haven't been in real fights. That's all good. You may never be in vicious fight and praise God. But I'm talking about the kind of fight were you will fight your mama, your daddy or the memory of them that threatens to take you out! That's psychological warfare in dealing with damaged goods. You increase your warfare sparing them. The memory may linger on but God can remove the pain or the sting of the ordeal. Jesus said 'Suppose ye that I am come to give peace on earth? I tell you, Nay; but rather division: For from henceforth there shall be five in one house divided, three against two, and two against three.' (Luke 12:51, 52) That's war! Realize I mean fight in prayer because some things and some people you can't cut off. God gives you wisdom in dealing with each situation especially when it comes to loved ones and close associates.

Once a relative whom I love dearly brought some stolen goods of immense value to my house and I called the police. If they ever stole again, I can tell you that they didn't dare bring it to my house. It's called 'Tough Love'. You got to have spiritual tough love too. The Bible says *if a man strengthens the hand of the evil doer, evil shall never part from his house.* (Prov. 17:13) That goes for a church house, a business and even a nation. We must war through prayer and get the victory before a relationship or situation gets out of control. But if it is out of control you still need apostolic interventions and angelic assistance. Use wisdom for each situation is unique. I know the scripture say *'Love covers a multitude of sins.'* This verse is talking about the agape love of God as we continue to pray and love people in Christ but even so we have to maintain integrity and character as we love them and God will direct our path.

I was a 'Tomboy' when I was growing up. I had all brothers, no sisters, nine uncles and many male cousins. One day my oldest brother along with other guys went to fight a rivalry gang and unbeknown to him, when he got there, I showed up too. He tried to make me go home and I refused. I had a stick nearly bigger than me. His friends told him to make me go home. He said I tried and I can't do anything with her. So one of the big tough guys thought he would teach me a lesson that I was no match for the fight that was about to go down. Suddenly he grabbed me by my wrist! And I remember to this day that I absolutely could not move. He stared me down in my face but I stared him back down.

Unable to move, and seemingly over-powered, my mind was still saying: If my brother's going to fight so am I and your weapon of intimidation will not stop me! Fortunately the opposing gang did not show up. My brother and his cohorts may have lost the battle just trying to protect me. You see, you got to beat a person in their mind before you can beat them in their spirit. That's why the enemy wars against our mind. The mind is a battleground! No one had told me prior to going that I could not win. If you got this book in your hand, you're a winner and God is raising you up as a warrior to kick a cage door in, go in and fight a lion, a tiger and a bear to set the captive free!

War for your loved ones! War for that prophetic word! War for your Destiny! For effective warfare, you got to walk in a high level of integrity and character to war on this realm. It's classified as high level warfare because you are exposed to much more frontline fire. If you don't walk in integrity, if you don't walk in love, if you don't walk in the Spirit the devil will knock you down! He will say Peter, Paul and Jesus I know, but who are you? (See Acts 19:14) He's taking entire churches out even Mega churches have had to close their doors. The scriptures say *smite the shepherd and scatter the sheep!* (Mark 14:27) Zechariah 1:14-21 describes a scattering. This story can be compared to the corporate scattering of a church illustrating the urgency to stay on the wailing-wall in travailing, prevailing and intercessory prayer.

THE SCATTERING

So the angel that communed with me said unto me, Cry thou, saying, Thus saith the LORD of hosts; I am jealous for Jerusalem and for Zion with a great jealousy. And I am very sore displeased with the heathen that are at ease: for I was but a little displeased, and they helped forward the affliction. ...I am returned to Jerusalem with mercies: my house shall be built in it...and a line shall be stretched forth upon Jerusalem. Cry yet, saying...My cities through prosperity shall yet be spread abroad; and the LORD shall yet comfort Zion, and shall yet choose Jerusalem. Then lifted I up mine eyes, and saw, and behold four horns. And I said unto the angel that talked with me, What be these? And he answered me, These are the horns which have scattered Judah, Israel, and Jerusalem. And the LORD shewed me four carpenters. Then said I, What come these to do? And he spake, saying, These are the horns which have scattered Judah, so that no man did lift up his head: but these are come to fray them, to cast out the horns of the Gentiles, which lifted up their horn over the land of Judah to scatter it.

Though God loved the nation of Israel, there was still a scattering. Yet God in his mercy returned to repair the breaches illustrated by the carpenters who came to cast out the enemy. As Intercessors on behalf of the church we are carpenters. God is a repairer of the breach and a restorer of the path and He calls us repairers of the breach. (see Is. 58:12) We have to tear down the altars of Baal, rebuild the altars of God. Where the fire is still lit we just need to keep it lit like the priest who kept the candle burning day and night in the temple. We are not just reigning as kings but we are presiding as priest too. (See Rev. 1:6) We keep the home fire burning in our hearts through prayer, love and faith. We have world overcoming faith. This is the victory which overcomes the world even our faith. In this spiritual war we are in we war from a victorious realm. (See Eph. 2:6, 1 John 5:4)

The Bible says in **Revelation 12** 'And there was War in heaven and Michael and his angels fought against the dragon and his angels.' The Word didn't say the dragon's demons. The word of God says his angels. So you got to be careful about some of them angels you're seeing. Whatever you're seeing needs to line up with the word of God because Satan can transform himself as an angel of light. If you are walking in darkness or caught up with sin in your life then some of those angels you are seeing just might be demons. But thank God we do have angelic assistance warring on our behalf in heavenly places against the powers of darkness.

Revelation 12 goes on to say that the Dragon and his angels were thrown out by Michael the Prince and his angels! Glory to God! Jehovah Gibbor! Our Commander in Chief! Lord of the Armies of Heaven! The Lord of Host is His name! As I engaged in high level warfare God spoke to me in a prophetic dream in a powerful voice and said 'Michael Is Here!' That is the anointing of Michael the archangel. We have the anointing to stand! The angels were dispatched to do war on behalf of Daniel the prophet and the nation of Israel. (See Daniel 10:13) And God is still dispatching His angels to do war on behalf of his people.

THE ARCH RAINBOW

MICHAEL IS HERE!

One evening we were coming from Chicago riding on Highway 94. The weather was clear. Then we passed through an area called Lawrence. I saw a huge rainbow in the sky. I was fascinated by it! I tried to capture it with my camera but the battery was weak and did not flash. Nor did the camera pick up the rainbow so I thought until I downloaded the pictures to my computer. As we got closer the rainbow was not just to the left of us but it was a huge arch that went across the entire highway or sky above the highway. I tell you it was totally awesome! I marveled at such majesty and grandeur displayed! It was beautiful! I had never seen anything like it in my life neither had anyone traveling with me in the car. The weather was slightly cloudy yet clear-like. Immediately when we passed under the rainbow, the weather took on a drastic change and the sky grew dark and eerie. The weather worsened with black clouds looming above and a strange darkness over shadowed the area and the rainbow was gone. Later on I did some research on the rainbow. This is some of what I found: I called the display 'The Arch Rainbow.'

> **Arch**…is symbolic of transcendence; that is, passing from the bounds of the earthly to the heavenly. (Job 22:14, Amos 9:6) **Rainbow**: a symbol of the Creator's covenant of perpetuity and prosperity with the earth.[9] **Rainbow** stands for covenant. There is a passing going on from the earthly to the heavenlies; from fleshly, carnality to full of the spirit by power. Transformation is on the horizon. God's covenant promises are about to be manifested. The promise of prosperity is on the horizon. It will get darker before this coming dawn but we must keep traveling, too make it through. There will be time travel in quantum leaps through

transition. **Arch** as in Archangel- the term for the chief or ruling angels of God's creation. Michael and Gabriel are archangels.[10]

We were on our way back from KEGAN, the Apostolic Prophetic conference in Chicago when we saw this rainbow. One of the prophetic words spoken at the conference was from the scripture in Hebrews 13:14 *'For here have we no continuing city, but we seek one to come.'* 'He's disconnecting them from an earthly city and connecting them to a heavenly city, the New Jerusalem. He's doing away with the old order. In this war you got to go by what God is doing in the kingdom not by what you see.' We walk by faith. I believe the arch rainbow that we saw symbolizes a strengthening or strength; to strengthen for what is to come. Later, another prophetic word from the same source of the conference said: 'You can't afford to sit down and lose momentum at this time.' And for double impact again God said to me 'Michael the Archangel Is Here!' Thank God for angelic assistance those warring angels that war on our behalf as we prevail in prayer to see the fulfillment of prophecy and our destiny.

The **Full Armor of God** is also available for us to war with as we prevail in prayer. *For we wrestle not against flesh & blood but against principalities, against powers, against the rulers of the darkness of this world, against spiritual wickedness in high places. (Eph. 6:10)* God has not given us the spirit of fear, but of power, love and a sound mind. The 'Helmet of salvation' helps to guard that sound mind to withstand the psychological fire of warfare. The 'breastplate of righteousness' lets the devil know when he accuses us that 'God is our righteousness! And we are the righteousness of God created in Christ Jesus for his workmanship. We use the 'Sword of the Spirit' to wield the word of God against the forces of evil that combat to take the prophetic word. Tell the devil 'this book of the law shall not depart out of my mouth by I shall meditate in it day and night and then shall my way be successful and prosperous! The 'Shield of faith' quenches all those flaming darts of fire the enemy hurls at your mind, body, spirit and soul.

Our loins must be girded about with 'the Spirit of Truth' to guard against the spirit of error, the spirit of divination and what I call D-angels—demons transforming themselves into angels of light. The

Spirit of Truth is our Helper in this war, our Comforter, the Companion and He will bring us into all Truth. Our feet must be strapped with the gospel of peace able to speed us on in due season. (See Eph. 6) We have to ask God for a greater outpouring of discernment and wisdom so we will know when to hold, know when to fold, know when to walk away and know when to run in this war. Not defect but run the race set before us. (See 1 Co. 9:24)

God is looking for faithful people. God says too kill the giant! The giant that is within! Some of us do quite a good job at going after the enemy without and shrink back in the face of the enemy within. He initially tried to keep you from coming to Jesus but he lost that battle. He also wants to keep you from the cross. The cross exposes sin. Whether it looks like it or not he's lost that battle too. Jesus said take up your cross and follow me. (Mark 8:34) That is allowing him to be Lord in your life as well as Savior too. God is looking for spiritual warriors who will be obedient and learn to take the fire of being ostracized, the rejection, the hatred and every other offence and opposition that we encounter on this journey. (See Matt. 10, 23) He wants you functioning as a wise worshipping warrior who will learn to distinguish whose voice is talking to you at any given time so you can know who inspired your thoughts. The heart can be exceedingly deceptive leading to unnecessary warfare in individual lives, entities, even war of nations which we will discuss in the next chapter part two of prevailing prayer. God wants all of our heart and don't kid yourself like I did once, only God knows when He's got it.

HIGH LEVEL SPIRITUAL WARFARE!

7

GAPS AND OPEN DOORS

One night I went to bed feeling quite spiritual. Not just religious but super spiritual if you will. I had been reading, studying, worshipping and praying. I remember covering my mind and my dreams but the devil got in anyway. I have a gift of prophetic dreaming but the battle had gotten so rough I had to cover my mind, my ear gate and especially my dreams under the blood of Jesus to ward off satanic transformation. Initially upon awaking, I didn't even know that I had been dreaming. Suddenly as I sat there I remembered that I had been dreaming. I began to dwell on the dream and try to figure out how Satan got in. There seemed to be no open door that I knew of. Then I felt like this was unfair. Perhaps I forgot the scripture that says *'let him who think he standeth take heed lest he suddenly fall.' (1st Co 10:12)* So I said in a sorrowful tone Lord this is so unfair. My mind was on you when I went to bed. How could this happen?

Suddenly a strong impression was impressed upon me that God does not have ALL of my heart and that was how Satan got in. There I was determined to stop him and he got in anyway. I know you can stop Satan's attacks. I've done that successfully before even his attacks in my dreams. But now the stakes were higher the fire heated up seven times revealing matters of the heart that I knew not of. For He did say in his word no man can know the heart prime reason for the continual guard. When I pray I confess sin known and unknown, commission and omission and the sins of my fathers to ward off operation of generational curses but thank God: *Where sin abound grace abound the more. (Gal. 5:20)* God told me there is a difference from what comes merely from your head from what comes from your heart. Some things come from the heart and others are like pop ups on the internet and merely come from the head. But pop ups will try to take control. If you have computer experience you know this.

We have to know where we are coming from to war effectively. I was now able to 'see another law in my members, warring against the law of my mind, and bringing me into captivity...' (Rom. 7:23) For the word of God is quick, and powerful...a discerner of the thoughts and intents of the heart... (see Eph. 6:6) We can't do God's will merely from the head. His will must be done in humility from the heart and in the Spirit because when the taskmaster of trial, tribulation and temptation come they will try you as fire! We have to be like the apostle during the hot winds of persecution 'Serving the Lord with all humility of mind...with many tears, and temptations... (See Acts 20:19)

The purification process goes on. Daniel 11:34 says: 'And some of them of understanding shall fall, to try them, and to purge, and to make them white, even to the time of the end: because it is yet for a time appointed.' So we are troubled on every side, yet not distressed, perplexed, but still we do not despair. (See 2 Cor. 4:8) For the Lion of Judah has triumphed and prevailed over all the forces of the enemy. '...having spoiled principalities and powers, he made a show of them openly, triumphing over them in it. (Col. 2:15) Even when the war becomes vicious we are victorious because of the triumph of the Lamb. The victory is in Christ Jesus. We keep on pressing! Onward Christian soldiers! We are given the keys to the kingdom of heaven to wage effective war with. (see Matt. 16:19) Jesus said in Luke 10:19 'behold I give you power...over all the power of the enemy and nothing shall by any means hurt you'.

Yet, there are times when you may feel like you've been picked out to be picked on. Handpicked by God can mean hand-targeted by the devil. The enemy is after the Christ seed in you just like he was when he moved Herod to slaughter the babies in Jerusalem. He doesn't want the image of Christ to be formed in you. He doesn't want you to come into your spiritual inheritance as a Son of God. First John 3:8 says '...for this purpose the Son of God was manifested, that he might destroy the works of the devil.' When you walk in the room the enemy is only intimidated by your presence. But the manifestation of Christ presence in you causes devils to be driven out! You become a serious threat to the kingdom of darkness when

Christ presence in you is manifested. It's the yoke destroying presence of the anointing of God. The weapons of our warfare are not carnal but are mighty through God to the pulling down of strongholds in our lives, communities and the nations. God wants us to intercede for our nation, for governmental officials, law enforcement, schools, churches, businesses and every other aspect of our communities. For, our country is not only in a physical war but a spiritual war too.

NATION AT WAR

As we intercede on behalf of foreign mission work we must continue to pray for the soul of our nation too. The importance of praying for our country was reinforced in me one night as I watched the PBS documentary '**GOD IN AMERICA**'. The documentary had six episodes. I will recapitulate the main thought that I took away from the program. One commentator (speaking about Dr. Martin Luther King Jr.) said something to this effect: 'you can't be the king and a prophet on the outside too throwing pebbles like Jeremiah.' It was also said that America is becoming ever more a pluralistic society with many different cultures and religions. The President and society would like to move to a 'respect' of all religion with more tolerance—a nation of many different gods with respect to one another. There's a call for a nation pluralistic and at the same time a call for those who believe in One God too.

The question is: How can a nation be pluralistic and under one God too? When comparing the two the nation has to be one or the other. It has to be a pluralistic nation under many gods. Or it is a monotheistic nation under one God. Plural and one are opposite each other. The only way they can exist together is to compromise. The Bible says how can two walk together except they agree? On one end of the spectrum you got Communism with **no gods**. The other extreme is 'pluralism and one God merged' to **all gods** included. America is beginning to look more and more like the Tower of Babel spoken of in the 11th chapter of the Book of Genesis.

At the Tower of Babel the people were under one tongue but they became pluralistic tongues when God stepped in and separated them. Our attempt is the opposite to have pluralism (many tongues) and to be unified as one at the same time. As I said the very term pluralism goes against the reality of one. You can't have them both. I understand the human logic of tolerance behind acceptance and pluralism but it is impossible to mix 'true' Christianity. This 'American thing' called something special in the documentary, that uniqueness that backed the American Revolution and helped formed the First Amendment is not so unique after all. There is nothing new under the sun according the Ecclesiastes writer.

The **New Age** religion embracing spirituality without Christ sovereignty fails to help. The very core of Christianity is that there is only One God. If you take away the core you remove the 'Christ' out of Christianity. In pluralism and interfaith you kill the concept of One God. You also kill the concept of pluralism if you embrace a God that says He is the only God. In the doctrine of Inclusiveness you lose the concept of the judgment. Therefore you have to reform Christianity. Christianity might be up for reform among some Christian churches but the God of Abraham, Isaac and Jacob is not. Neither or the views of Jesus and the Apostles regarding hell, the devil, the works of the devil, iniquity and judgment. So this special thing, this uniqueness is nothing more than the new man with an old heart trying to carve out a new existence: Life on planet earth without God! That is the God who was bold enough to say there is no other God besides me! (See Mark 12:32)

THE CHURCH PREVAILING AGAINST THE GATES OF HELL

Thus 'true' Christianity's main profession and that of God's church is that there is only One God—the God who made the heavens and the earth. The foundation of Christian doctrine is under attack. Our church is at war and our nation is at war too. But the 'true church' of God will prevail against this attempt of coup d'état. I was dreaming prophetically one night when I saw and heard things regarding martyrdom, purpose, etc. *God revealed some things to me. He impressed upon me that there is no need for the saints to worry in this warfare. He knows all things concerning us and will keep us'.* Worry is a son of fear. I woke up from that dream empowered! Full of faith and inoculated against the spirit of fear and the powers of hell!

The gates of hell are attempting to prevail against the modern day church in this generation we are living in. We are like Pergamos the church where Satan's seat is. Speaking to the saints at Pergamos, the Lord said in Revelation 2:13 *'I know thy works, and where thou dwellest, even where Satan's seat is: and thou holdest fast my name, and hast not denied my faith, even in those days… (of) martyr(dom)…* So I saw martyrdom in the dream and martyrdom doesn't always have to be physical. You can also be spiritually martyred. Some people think martyrdom doesn't happen in the United States. Well God says it does. But more so spiritually than in nations were Christians are physically persecuted and killed. But we have seen martyrdom rise here in the West. Even when a minister commits suicide we are well aware somehow the enemy had him where Satan's seat is even if it was only in his mind. War prevailing against a church is depicted by the following dream I called:

TRAIN WRECK!

In the dream I stood in astonishment from a distance witnessing and observing a massive train wreck! There were others all around looking on too. The wreckage scene was tremendous! I gazed in awe at this scenario as I said 'I've never seen a train wreck before!' When the train wrecked some of the rail cars went one way and some of the cars went the other way. They went in different directions. Also when the train wrecked some of the rail cars were still going as though they were still linked up and nothing had happened but they were bound for impact! The engine also looked unaffected but it was bound for impact too! I don't know what caused the wreckage but it appears that the train was hit in the middle!

The train represents the church in spiritual warfare. The engine represents the Leader and leadership. The railcars are also leadership and lay members too. The middle is the belly, intercession the place symbolizing the power of the Spirit. A spiritual Tsunami hit the church! What church you say? You already know. Read the headlines. That's why we must be aware that we are engaged in spiritual warfare. High level warfare calls for Special Forces and intercession to prevail in prayer. Like the military calling in the Air Force when they want to do an air raid and annihilate the forces below. As warriors we are strategically positioned to do battle. We war from the victorious realm where we are seated in Christ Jesus at the right hand of the Father. (Eph. 2:6) We do not war against people. Our battle is not with flesh and blood but with principalities, powers, and rulers of the darkness of this world. If we forget these important points and tactics we can end up like the train above wrecked!

God said in Matthew 16:18 '...upon this rock I will build my church; and the gates of hell shall not prevail against it'. The gates of hell will not prevail against the 'true' church of God that is seated in Christ Jesus in heavenly places. A good source on spiritual warfare is 'The Church That Refused to Die' by Pastor Roger L. Fredrikson. He does not talk about spiritual warfare per se but he takes you through the miraculous rebuilding and restoration of a church after spiritual war. The church was 4000 members strong. After the war was over there were only 400 left but at least the rebels had walked the plank and the restoration and rebuilding could move forward.

I watched episode 2 of '**A STORY ABOUT US**' a very inspiring documentary on the Revolution aired on PBS. They talked about freedom as a dream saying if you want your dream to come true you have to fight for it! Sometimes this may mean new weapons, tactics, discipline, intelligence, etc. I also took note the emergency meeting of the signing of the Declaration was rooted in belief in God. One commentator said that attitude in war means a lot to as a weapon. The mind is the great battlefield because it can come under attack. In spiritual war if you're thinking is not inspired by God then it is induced by the flesh, the world, or the devil. *The Bible says 'But the unbelieving Jews stirred up the Gentiles, and made their minds evil affected against the brethren'. (Acts 14:2)*

In the documentary at one point during a harsh winter Washington's men at Valley Forge were dying because the Congress hadn't given them adequate provision. I saw this in spiritual warfare such as not having adequate spiritual food whether it is a lack of prayer, loving fellowship, lack of teaching of the word of God, faith, etc. We too need adequate provision else the morale will fall low. The troops will become tired and needless casualties result. Thank God for effective five-fold ministries being in operation that succor and help equip the saints. Though we war against wicked spirits in heavenly places, we are more than conquerors. (See Rom. 8:37) The following names are some wicked spirits to combat and war against in warfare prayer:

> The spirit of **Athaliah**: She is devastating. She kills her own seed. (See 2nd Chron. 22:10)
>
> The spirit of **Jezebel** with her sorceries, witchcraft, control, manipulation, domination, divination and sexual seduction; (See 1, 2 Kings)
>
> The **Python** spirit a spirit of divination that seeks to overwhelm, choke the life out and swallow up blessings; (see Acts 16:16)
>
> **Leviathan** a proud high-minded, stiff-neck spirit; (see Is. 29:1)
>
> The **Anaconda** the largest viper in the world
>
> War against **Cold Love**; (Mat. 24:12)
>
> **Familiar spirits**: such as the spirit of Korah or Absalom; (See Joshua 7)
>
> The spirit of **Achan** and **Filthy lucre;** lying, greed, disobedience (see Joshua7, Tit. 1:11)
>
> All Images of Jealousy and **Idolatry**, etc.[11]

God said it is time out for **SELECTIVE LOVE** in the church and we need to intensify consecration. We got to clean up our mess, get the sin out and get the house in order. Or He is going to come through the church and roar like a Lion! The following dream depicts high level warfare against the church. (Also see Revelation twelve)

THE TWO GREAT DRAGONS

In the dream we were at a gathering maybe partly in the open and partly in a very large house. There was a woman there whose head was bent over in a paralyzed position and she was in pain. The apostolic was going forth in power as the Prophet laid hands on her and she was healed! So many people were present that needed to be ministered too. There were some disruptions to short circuit the service but the power of travailing, prevailing and intercessory prayer was going forth in power too! This was an awesome event when suddenly in the sky appeared a Great Dragon!

Then I looked to the other side of the sky and there appeared another Great Dragon. The dragons began shooting fire from their mouth toward us. People began to scatter! I suppose others who were prevailing in prayer did not flee at least not in the same manner as the other people. There was a man among us who had been sitting in the meeting and a small girl was with him.

Before the dragons manifested, the man had been told that a girl had been brutally raped but he didn't seem to care at all. After the commotion of the dragons shooting forth fire, the man got up to leave. He was not fleeing like the others. He simply walked calmly away as though nothing had occurred. And I saw his eyes and they were as pure evil. He was not one of us, not a true Christian. He was full of Satan; (dedicated to Satan as Apostle Martin would say, made up his mind to serve Satan. He had been masked as a wolf in sheep clothing.) I said no wonder he didn't care when he was told a little girl was brutally raped. In fact he had one with him. The dragon fire was still shooting and I woke up!

As I woke up that morning a strange thing occurred. I could hear lyrics of a song in my mind. I did not know the name of the song or who the artist was. Yet, I continued to hear some of the lyrics. I got on the internet and googled some of the lyrics. I kept coming up blank. I was not even sure the few lyrics that I kept hearing were really a song. But I finally found the link to the song on Youtube. As I listened to the song, I realized that I had never known who sang this song. Long ago, I had only heard it play on the radio at times. The name of the song was Sledgehammer. Some of the lyrics were: ...*You can have an Airplane flying if you bring your first car back. ...call me and I'll be anything you need. ...I wonna be your sledgehammer. ...this is my testimony...Put your mind at rest...Let there be no doubt about it...* Searching for the interpretation and the connection of this song to the dream of the Dragons, I did research and found out that the artist formed the group Genesis with an album title: From Genesis to Revelation. He played in a production called 7 angels of Rock with the opening song call Watcher of the Skies; wore a costume called

Magog; He did an album called The Lamb lies down on Broadway; Passion the soundtrack for The Last Temptation of Christ best New Age Performance Award. There was involvement in séances.[12] So I marveled at all the references to Christianity and the mixture. Yet that is not uncommon. For, many musicians have some kind of Christian background through parents, upbringing, etc. I was a stunned!

False religions, false doctrines, demonic influenced music and every other evil work are manifestation of the fire of the Dragon. I can just imagine a generation of young people swaying to the subliminal teachings of Satan going out all over the airwaves in the West. In the East the dragon represents fortune but in the West the dragon represents evil. Therefore, tolerance of 'pluralism embracing one God' symbolically speaking, is nothing more than the east mixing with the west, evil merging with good. Mixing religions causes characteristics to change causing catastrophic climatic shifts in the earth's atmosphere. We are certainly a nation at war in more ways than one. I saw in a prophetic dream about five years ago flood waters of great magnitude on the eastern border that reshaped the coastline. The Dragon also represents the following: *Leviathan, Dinosaur and Alligator*: *A high level of demonic attack; spiritual wickedness in high places; antichrist; Satan...cannot be tamed with the natural strength of man; principality; evil spirit; ancient demonic control; only the Lord has power over; dragon.*[13]

I also saw in a prophetic dream Fire! The fire spread across the land. Jesus said *'I came to send Fire on the earth...'* Even though He is the Prince of Peace to them who truly follow him, He came to send a sword of division against His enemies. (See Luke 12:49, 51, 52) The word of God says 'Up! Up! Deliver thyself from among them... from Babylon! Flee! Come Forth!' (See Zech. 2:6) God is still talking to the church today. He's saying don't mimic the world. Stop the mixture! '...come out from among them, and be ye separate, saith the Lord, and touch not the unclean thing; and I will receive you, (2nd Co 6:17) '...Save yourselves from this untoward generation'. (See Acts 2:40)

False religions, false teaching and cults as well as secular humanism are helping to make this an untoward generation. The Bible says purify your hearts you double-minded. (James 1:8, 4:8) Purified hearts are empowered to prevail in prayer. The world seeks to mix us and pull us away from God. The world says if you can't beat them, join them. You need a compromise gold card to join. The world is on an accelerated course. Technology is not the only thing rapidly advancing. Evil is advancing too. Up! Up! Deliver yourself…from Babylon! Do war with the prophecies that have gone on before you!

Here is a list of some anointing's to war with: the **Cyrus** anointing being heavenly commissioned, ordained and empowered to build. (See II Chron. 36:23); The Spirit of **Zerubbabel:** not by might, not by power but by the Spirit of the Lord the mountain that stands in the way of Christ's agenda is coming down. (See Zech. 4) **Repairers** of the Breach: the anointing for restoration and rebuilding. (See Is 58:12, Zech. 3); The **Joshua** warriors anointing; and, the **Jehu** anointing that was responsible for the destruction of Jezebel; all for the pulling down of strongholds, gaining ground and advancing the kingdom of God.

As God enlarges our territory we gain ground. We are atmosphere shifters even in hostile war environments. In order to maintain climate control we must maintain momentum. Too often we gain ground and lose it. The stakes may rise higher, but the way we got it, is how we keep it. Just like in the natural the spoils of war and territory gained by a nation must be governed and maintained. So it is in spiritual war the ground must be maintained by our daily faith walk and governed by God. Living in a fallen world makes this necessary as the warfare intensifies and the environment becomes hostile. The warfare was so intense Apostle Paul said he fought beast at Ephesus!

Daniel encountered spiritual violence when he was thrown into the Lion's den. The enemy wanted him so bad he went to extreme lengths to get him but God delivered him. I call it Spiritual Entrapment. The spirit of Jezebel seeks to kill the prophets. She killed God's prophets and exalted her false prophets. But Obadiah is an example of marketplace ministry. Even though he worked for a wicked king who had a wicked wife, Obadiah was courageous enough to hide 100 of God's prophets in a cave. This was told to Elijah the prophet whom Jezebel was wicked enough to threaten too.

The Apostle Paul talked about the great cloud of witnesses of faith that we have. Some of them left this world without seeing the promise. Some were stoned, tempted, slain...they wandered about...being destitute, afflicted, tormented. (See Heb. 11:37) We are still in that same war only under a New Covenant. Jesus said in Matthew 10:17 'beware of men: for they will deliver you up...they will scourge you in their synagogues; ...but take heed the Holy Ghost will give you what to say in that hour.' Jezebel still seeks to kill the prophets and enslave the people of God. But we overcome by the blood of the lamb, the word of our testimony and we love not our lives unto the death...

Oftentimes we stop quoting this scripture at the end of the word testimony. But the days are coming and they are here that we got to love not our lives unto the death if it calls for standing up for Christ. Jesus said if you lose your life you will find it. If you find it, you will lose it. (See Mat. 10:39) We have no continuing city here. When we are delivered up, we must stand on the word, fight a good fight and keep the faith. Jesus said when the prince of this world comes he finds nothing in me. (See John 14:30) We are empowered to say the same thing as we stand on the Rock Jesus Christ.

In **Revelation 12** the Bible says and the dragon was wroth with the woman and went to do war with her seed... When the devil can't get you, he'll go after what you love. The world says a chain is only as strong as its weakest link. But 2nd Corinthians 12:10 says '...when I am weak, then am I strong.' God has chosen the foolish things of the world to confound the wise; and God hath chosen the weak things of the world to confound the things which are mighty. (1 Co. 1:27)

Jesus has commanded us to overcome this world and we overcome evil by good. The enemy wants you to get in the flesh, become like the evil that's coming against you, take matters into your own hands and avenge yourself. But God said vengeance is mine and I will repay! (Rom. 12:19) We work in cooperation with God as we do our part and He does His so don't become vengeful. Put on the Garments of Praise for a spirit of heaviness and bless God! God gives the oil of Joy for the spirit of mourning. Declare no weapon formed against me shall prosper! Every tongue that rises against me is condemned in judgment! Thank God for the beauty available for the ashes!

There are times in the heat of the battle God will empty out just to pour back in like reloading a weapon. As soldiers who are worshipping warriors, we are His weapons of warfare even if he has to reload us at times to destroy enemy forces. The thief comes to kill, steal and destroy. (See John 10:10) But his time is running out. Jesus came to give us life and life more abundantly, the increase. The enemy knows he has but a short time so he fights dirty. He will throw everything at you including the kitchen sink. He may have won some battles but we win the war. The word of God says …to continue in the faith, and that we must through much tribulation enter into the kingdom of God. (Acts 14:22)

Continue in prayer, and watch in the same with thanksgiving; (Col. 4:2) Pray Psalm 141:3 'Set a watch, O LORD, before my mouth; keep the door of my lips.' Contrary to what the world says talk is not cheap. The scriptures let us know that we can be ensnared by our own tongue. According to Proverbs 21:23 place a guard over your mouth and a watch over your tongue. Hold on to the horns of the altar! Guard your heart even in the midst of dragon fire. Your right at the moment of breakthrough! It's always darkest just before dawn.

**BLESSED ARE THE
WARRIORS THAT BELIEVED!**

8

HIGH NOON!

Throughout this book I discussed the critical need for greater awareness of spiritual warfare and the dual assignment of the intercessor at home and at the church. This prayer responsibility described as a two-fold burden is similar to carrying twins. I discussed how travailing, prevailing and intercessory prayer intertwine together to birth promise. Prevailing prayer gets the victory but you got to see that victory in your spirit first in order to get it. You got to hold on to what you see. One of the ways you hold on to what you see is through confession of faith. Confession of what you see. Calling those things that be not as though they were. (See Rom. 4:17) As you hang on to the altar in prayer, you need violent faith to see the prophetic promise emerge. At this point in your assignment it's like being great with child now, great with promise just breathing to come forth. The enemy knows this and sets up satanic barricades all the way down to the end. So as you approach the end of your assignment things can really start to get chaotic.

Due to the violent warfare encountered, like the apostle you may begin to feel like you are the one fighting beast at Ephesus. This is a potential hotbed for becoming battle worn and war weary. Or depressed like Elijah and run as a Jezebel hit is placed on your life. An assigned assassinator on your heels! Watch as well as pray! You don't want to end up hiding out in a cave of mixed emotions bound as a wounded warrior unable to move forward. It's a place of spiritual standoff! Showdown in limbo, which is nothing more than maintaining the status quo, mediocrity, hype, desperado and spiritual mirages of moves of God. Even at the end of war, war is still war! High Noon! Showdown at the O.K. Corral! Here is where you stand toe to toe with the devil, face the enemy of your soul and defeat his purpose against your destiny. The apostle stressed:

> For we would not, brethren, have you ignorant of our trouble which came to us in Asia, that we were pressed out of measure, above strength, insomuch that we despaired even of life: (2 Co. 1:8)

In these adverse conditions the stakes remain high as dark oppositional forces are encountered. Leviathan and the Anaconda are two of the most deadly foes to encounter in this war. You can't fight this battle on your own. If you try God says it's a battle you'll never forget! They are ancient foes who don't go down easy. The Anaconda is so huge and steeped in evil it looks preposterous! Leviathan beholds all high things: he is a king over all the children of pride. (See Job 41:34) Pray for God to put a hook in his jaw, to pierce his head and to slay that dragon! (See Job 4, Isa. 27:1) Even at this advanced stage in battle friendly fire still occurs and tempers can flare. Enemy arrows of accusation shoot forth and like Elijah, soldiers may become wounded, faltering under heavy artillery fire.

> Despite the carnage, the scripture says: 'who art thou that judgest another man's servant? For, a servant standeth or falleth to his own master.' (Rom. 14:4)

Making accurate judgment can be difficult through battle worn, war-weary eyes. We need to pray God send a fresh wind! We can't judge by appearance only but we must judge righteous judgment. (See Mat. 7:24) For, a righteous man falls seven times but he gets back up. Romans 14:4 goes on to say, 'that servant shall be held up for God is able to make us stand.' So regardless of the outcomes in war, God is still the Grand Weaver of our destiny. (See Ref. 17)

The strategy is to make a straight path. For the word of God says: make straight paths for yourselves, looking to Jesus the Author and Finisher of your faith who for the joy set before him endured the cross lest ye be weary and faint in your minds. (See Heb. 12) We got to endure our cross all the while holding on to what Jesus told Peter 'don't let your faith fail you!' We keep from fainting in our minds by allowing the mind of Christ to rule. The scripture tells us to acknowledge God in all our ways and He will make our paths straight. That is how we make a straight path for ourselves by acknowledging God in all our plans that He is the author of them. (See Prov. 3:6)

We come full circle in battle, on the verge of a new beginning, still in a spiritual war combatting for the full manifestation of the prophetic promise. We can't take down yet. We gained ground in this war but God wants more ground expansion of territory. For the kingdom of God is expanding. We can no longer sit still in a defensive position and merely hold the fort rejoicing only in what we obtained yesteryear. We got to change positions, come out of the cave of mediocrity. Using offensive warfare tactics storm the enemy's camp with the word of God, through prophetic prayer and by violent faith in the name of Jesus! We need strength! We're pushing out twins in this assignment! We need an adequate supply of endurance to birth them both.

The Bible says in Genesis 49:14 that Issachar was like an ass couched between two burdens with the strength and wisdom to deliver them both. The **sons of Issachar** also knew the times and the seasons. (see 1st Chron. 12:32) In a given situation we also need to know the time and the season. Is this the beginning or is this the end? Or are we still in the process? Under the heavy fire of trial and tribulation we can get tricked, deceived by the enemy who can transform himself into an angel of light to get us off track. (2 Cor. 11:14) Like the sons of Issachar we need to know accurate timing.

Timing was also a concern to the **Twelve Disciples**. They wanted to know what season they were really in. Their nation was under persecution, taxed, over-burdened and held captive by the Roman Empire. So they wanted to know the signs of the end. We can get so caught up in the artillery fire and offense that we get more focused on the end than we do on the One with the power to bring it to an end. Jesus called them 'hot winds of persecution!'

> *For there are those that shut up the kingdom of heaven against men...neither go in themselves, neither suffer them that are entering to go in. (Matt. 23:13)*

Jesus had to endure violent winds and contradictions of sinners and so may we. (see Heb. 12) Natural birthing as well as spiritual birthing is violent! Like a baby being delivered, we want out! Nature demands that the baby come out! God will put a demand on you. There is a demand on the anointing he has placed in your belly. We cry out for restoration and push to release! The fire is heated up sevenfold so we must turn up the level on fasting and prayer. This is like major surgery. It's a critical stage in battle. The enemy wants to pull the plug on destiny. That's why I said we must know the timing of God. It doesn't matter that you are at the end. The enemy will try to take you out at the 11th hour. Perhaps your deliverance is set for midnight. It's 11:58… There is such a thing as a lawful captive. (See Is. 49:24) Destiny hangs in the balance.

We see that during Jesus ministry, the nation of Israel desired restoration and release from captivity too but God was birthing His kingdom. God is still birthing His kingdom. He is birthing it in us— the kingdom of heaven is within. (Luke 17:21) The disciples asked Jesus was he going to restore things at that time. Basically they were saying we want to know! Are you going to deliver us now! I'm sure they had a method of deliverance already in mind too but rather than answering directly, Jesus taught them about the signs of the end times. All things have an end to them and the end of time as we know it is coming: The 'Ultimate Due Date' the Final Call! It's the Final payday when the Master of the House comes and shuts the door. That final day is coming. (See Luke 13:24-30) We don't want to get shut out. So in all we get, we need to get an understanding of the times and seasons we are really in and hold on to the horns of the altar free of contaminated prayer caused by contamination in the heart.

I say this because intense spiritual warfare can cause spiritual delirium but we don't have to succumb to spiritual mirages, persecution or false prophecy. Be wise as a serpent and harmless as a dove. The Ancient One of Days is still on our side. He's Lord of the Armies of heaven! The Lord told the angel, (speaking of the prophet Daniel) make this man to understand. We need understanding in the art of spiritual war. The stakes are high! As high as between death and life, heaven and hell and you got to know which one is speaking. There's a counterfeit that looks and sounds real. That's why he warned us not to judge merely by signs and wonders. (Mat. 24:24) He warns us in Mark 13:22, 'For false Christ's and false prophets shall rise, and shall shew signs and wonders, to seduce, if it were possible, even the elect.' Watch out! A spirit of seduction loosed in the land!

DAMSEL IN DISTRESS...

Spirits of seduction cause spiritual delusions and distress. There was a First Lady at a church I visited who seemed overly concerned that she might not make it in to heaven. For some reason she just could not get this scripture out of her mind: *'rejoice not in that the demons tremble but rejoice that your name is written down in the Lambs book of Life'*. (See Luke 10:20, Ph. 4:3, Rev 13:8) I didn't know she was distressed by this text until I went to the church and spoke. In the midst of speaking I said 'make sure your name is written down in the Lambs book of Life'. I didn't plan to say it. The words just came pouring out. Afterwards the pastor told the church how his wife had been plagued by this issue.

I also recalled that for years this same text had been a scripture that puzzled me. I was perplexed. Like Daniel the Lord had to make me understand. God told me that those people referred to in the text were sincerely going to believe that they were saved when they say to him Lord, Lord don't you know us? I don't know about you but that's a little scary to me. A spirit of delusion and deception are at work when you don't know the truth. The Lord will say to them depart from me ye workers of iniquity I know you not. (See Luke 13:27) Read the text in your Bible. He's not talking to sinners here. He's talking to people from the church. And we know what iniquity is. It is sin. They were workers of lawlessness. Heaven is real but everybody's not going. Despite interfaith and inclusive teaching, everybody is not included. The following story was told to me in regards to the:

LAMB'S BOOK OF LIFE

There was a Pastor who was sick. She enquired of God as she wanted to know was her name in The Book. (I suppose just in case the day of reckoning had come and she had to get her house in order.) She had a dream. ***In the dream the Lord told her that her name was not written in the Lamb's Book of Life.***

The pastor told the dream she had to another preacher. The pastor had to get it right before she left this world and she left early. Saints of old used to sing 'GET RIGHT CHURCH AND LET'S GO HOME!' It was not this new stuff of compromise and inclusion with watered down theology that treats Gods love, mercy and grace like it's cheap. It's called the hyper grace message. Hebrews 10:2 says Of how much sorer punishment, suppose ye, shall he be thought worthy, who hath trodden underfoot the Son of God, and hath counted the blood of the covenant, wherewith he was sanctified, an unholy thing, and hath done despite unto the Spirit of grace? (See 1st Tim. 4:2, Rom 1:28, 2 Tim. 3:8, Jude 1:4, 1st Pet. 4:3) God spoke to me in a dream and said:

> 'AT THE END OF THE DAY WHAT MATTERS MOST IS DID YOU LIVE HOLY?'

You are not living holy, if you are living in habitual sin. The stakes are higher now. You got some churches supporting sin and calling it holy convocation but its' still sin. When it's all said and done, after we've finished preaching, teaching, witnessing, singing, etc. we want to make sure our name is written down in the Lambs book of Life too. Paul said I keep under my body, and bring it into subjection: lest that by any means, when I have preached to others, I myself should be a cast away. (1st Cor. 9:27) We are sojourners in this world but we are not of this world. We can't just get with the times and move according to the spirit of the world. We got to have a dressing room mentality of a virgin Bride and get it right, keep it right and walk in it right before that last trumpet sound. We need the strength of God and the wisdom of our Lord.

WISDOM IS A DEFENSE

Wisdom is a fortified defense. In Matthew the 25th chapter, Jesus was discussing the (signs of the end of the world) with his disciples on Mount Olive when he put forth a parable to them: He compared the Kingdom of Heaven to '**Ten Virgins**' five of them wise and five of them foolish. All ten of them being engaged to be married prepared themselves and went out to meet the bridegroom. The five foolish virgins brought their lamps with them but for some reason they forgot to bring oil. A Lamp is a vessel. And just like a car needs gas a vessel needs oil in it to operate according to the original manufacturers specifications. Not the specifications of the times! So the five wise virgins brought their oil with them and the five foolish virgins brought none. Throughout that night all ten of them slept and slumbered, when suddenly the bridegroom came and the five foolish virgins were not ready. They tried to borrow some oil from the wise virgins but they only had enough oil for themselves. The five wise virgins told the foolish virgins to go and buy their own oil.

However, time had run out for them all. The end of Time as we know it... It was the Final call. The onset of the eleventh hour had passed, approaching midnight fast and suddenly the real Master of the House came. The one whose name is Faithful and True! (Rev. 19:11) The Bridegroom showed up and it was too late. He told the five foolish virgins that He didn't even know them. Their names were not found in the Lambs book of Life. We can't afford to be foolish. How can you see someone who doesn't have any light?

The light is symbolic of Christ like, faithful, true and walking in love and the fruit of the Spirit. The son of man came to expose the works of darkness. He didn't come to die on a cross so you could have liberty to keep on walking in darkness. That is why the adversary works so hard to put the light out. The devil wants to maintain his wicked position of authority. Apostle J. B. Woods said that God revealed to her that the ten virgins represent 100% of the church. 50% of the church will not be ready. (See Ref. 18) The church in the west got to repent and do their first works again. They are like that rich church the Laodiceans spoken of in Revelations having also lost the fear of the Lord in the name of science, secularism, materialism, denominationalism and humanism.

As members of the body of Christ we are the vessels. The oil is symbolic of the dunamis power of the Holy Ghost. We got to be full of the baptism of the Holy Ghost. We got to be showered again through times of refreshing. A continuous supply of the Holy Ghost is needed to fortify and keeps us. We must be able to withstand the warfare, the trials, persecution adverse situations and tribulation and we can't do it without the fullness of the Holy Spirit.

God showed me revelation of the 'End Times' in a vision one night. The Bible says that in the last days knowledge shall increase and they shall go to and fro. Seal up the book until the end! (See Daniel 12:4) I think we all would agree that knowledge has accelerated in our times. Push a button and get almost any information you want. But knowledge is different from eating from the Tree of Life. We got a challenge as we work out our on soul salvation: feelings, and facts versus walking in the Truth. We walk in the truth by walking in the Word and His Spirit despite the warfare. We are not alone. We got the Lord on our side. Jesus said 'I'll never leave you nor forsake you. Lo I am with you even unto the end of the world.' Gird up your loins with the Spirit of Truth! Spiritual war can cause you to feel like you're at the end of the world, but you're not at the end of the world. You're at the end of the trial. In great pain crying out, ready to deliver, ready to birth the promise.

We must remain proactive on the offensive warpath. We can't just sit around and wait for the promise to drop in our lap. Like the four lepers declare: why sit here until we die? (See 2 Ki 7:2) There is resurrection power after all the hell you been through. There is abundant life on the other side of the fire! All the warfare that I personally encountered was illustrated to me *in a night vision where I saw myself fly over a Towering Furnace of Fire! As I flew over the fire, I said, 'I ain't no bird!'* I know that I meant I bleed red blood too when cut.

It's about matters of the heart where the heart is being circumcised in the refiner's fire. Spiritually speaking God will circumcise our heart on the eight day cutting out the contaminants. It's a painful process that may seem like a long struggle. Like Jacob wrestling with the angel at Peniel all night long. (See Gen. 32)

One evening, I was looking at the movie Joseph the King of Dreams. I had seen the movie before. I never paid much attention to the song in the past but this time the lyrics brought tears to my eyes as he sang: *'you know better than I. You know the way... let go of the need to know why for you know better than I. I saw a bird and thought that I could follow but it was you who taught that bird to fly...'* His eye is still on the sparrow. I know this from the Logos word and the prophetic word. For in the midst of the warfare God spoke a word to me and said MY EYE IS ON THE SPARROW. I had wrestled with the need to know why so much warfare and pain. Especially at a time when it seems everyone was teaching only prosperity and wealth.

Even the kingdom message began to take on the same tone. So all the warfare seemed so unnecessary but warfare is a threshing floor experience where only God has the answers to your pain. No cute, quick cliché can heal it. Like Daniel in the Lion's Den, God alone is the Deliverer in every trial. Going through is just what it says you are going through not pitching a tent there. Paraphrasing Dr. Martin Luther King Jr. 'we've seen some difficult days...' Days that seem like a messenger from Satan comes to buffet you but look at what the Apostle says about these trying days in 2nd Corinthians:

> '...lest I should be exalted above measure through the abundance of the revelations, there was given to me a thorn in the flesh, the messenger of Satan to buffet me, lest I should be exalted above measure. For this thing I besought the Lord thrice, that it might depart from me. And he said unto me, My grace is sufficient for thee: for my strength is made perfect in weakness. Most gladly therefore will I rather glory in my infirmities, that the power of Christ may rest upon me. Therefore I take pleasure in infirmities, in reproaches, in necessities, in persecutions, in distresses for Christ's sake: for when I am weak, then am I strong.' (2nd Corinthians 12:7-10)

Often we quote the apostle when he said, I didn't come in lofty words but I came to you in the demonstration of power. But he also came in humility and meekness like the Lamb of God. Paul said *I came to you in fear, weakness and in trembling. (1 Cor. 2:3)* This position helps us to stay humble when God exalts us. This messenger of Satan which comes to buffet can cause you to feel like you are not only at the gates of hell but in hell itself. But agree with the psalmist who said if I make my bed in hell He is there! (Ps. 139:8) He is our Deliverer. That's how love goes. Love straightens it out. Love redeems and reconciles us to walk in agreement. Love is also a two way street. As Jesus was going to his cross, he asked his disciple: 'Peter do you Love me? ...Then...' (See John 21:15) You know the rest of the story. We say we love Him but when it comes to bearing our cross we got to put our name there too. All in true love is fair.

BLESSED ARE THE WARRIORS THAT BELIEVED!

At the beginning of your spiritual walk, when you first repented God spoke to your spirit man and said let there be light and there was light. You were born again into the kingdom of God. When trials come, each trial is like a death and resurrection. When one trial ends the new life comes, the new beginning. We still live in a fallen world but we walk closer and closer to the Light. Jesus said if the salt loses his savor wherewith the world be seasoned. (See Mat. 5:13) Have salt in yourselves—He commanded. Here it is again we must work out our own soul salvation in fear and trembling. This responsibility can't be left to anyone else. It's all a part of spiritual warfare as you maintain the single eye focus of faith.

We are part of a kingdom that has no end so keep on praying, keep on asking, keep on knocking and keep on seeking until God answers your prayer. You've experienced the trauma of war. Like Israel in the days of Elijah, you've seen days of nakedness, drought and famine. You've come through category 5 storms and prevailed! You fought the good fight of faith as you held on to God's word. Now your time is coming to walk in the manifestation of abundant rain. Let's see what the prophet says in 1st Kings 18: 41-46:

> 'And Elijah said unto Ahab, **Get thee up**, eat and drink; for there is a sound of abundance of rain. So Ahab went up to eat and to drink. And Elijah went up to the top of Carmel; and he cast himself down upon the earth, and put his face between his knees, And said to his servant, Go up now, look toward the sea. And he went up, and looked, and said, **There is nothing**. And he said, Go again seven times. And it came to pass at the seventh time, that he said, Behold, there ariseth a little cloud out of the sea, like a man's hand. And he said, Go up, say unto Ahab, Prepare thy chariot, and get thee down, that the rain stop thee not. And it came to pass in the meanwhile, that the heaven was **black** with clouds and wind, and there was a great rain....'

I used to long for an Elijah just like the nation of Israel did in the days of Roman captivity. You can read about that longing in my book 'Rivers of Waters'. I no longer long for Elijah. Elias has already come. (See Mark 9:13) Jesus said if you can receive it then receive it. Words of prophecy spoken in due season propel us into destiny. It's knowledge that catapults you forward to prevail in prayer as you war for your prophetic word. The enemy doesn't want you to prevail in prayer for after the pain comes the abundant rain—the gainful expansion of God's kingdom.

God will show you some things in the spirit that you can't see in the natural. It seems impossible! But *'When You See the Invisible you are empowered to do the Impossible'. (Ref. 19)* Jesus said in Mark 10:27 '...with men it may be impossible but with God all things are possible.' Build by what God shows you. Walk by faith and not by sight. War with the prophecies gone on before you! Like Jesus, work as you see your Father work. What is our work? It's to have faith and believe on Jesus whom the Father has sent. (See John 6:29) The scripture says in Luke's gospel, chapter 1:45 'Blessed is she that believed for there shall be a performance of the things told to her from the Lord'.

It doesn't matter what your gender is you can put your name there too. Faith is the substance of things hoped for and the evidence of things not seen. (See Heb. 11:1) You don't see it yet? Brace yourself like Elijah on your knees in prayer. Go and look again. Like Elijah's servant for a while you saw nothing in the natural. All you had was a promise and a prayer and the devil tried with all his might with the host of hell to take that. Yet you continued to persevere and work diligently not only to birth your own promise but the corporate burden too. Time went on and then you saw a little sign. Then as time further progressed you saw a larger manifestation. Stand in faith and take it forward! Now is the time!

The heavens are open and it is time for the abundance of rain—meanwhile, the text goes on to say, just before the rain pours down, the heavens became black with clouds and wind... That can symbolize the chaos that breaks out at the end of the assignment in the 11th hour to divert you and abort destiny. As Elijah warned the King, don't let it stop you! The kingdom of heaven suffereth violence but the violent taketh it by force. Fight in the spirit, fight and win. You wake up the next day and it's still going on fight again! Declare 'I shall not be cheated out of my Inheritance! The Lord is on our side. He is Jehovah-Gibbor our commander in chief.' Even though dark clouds loom and stormy winds blow a great rain is coming! Ushering in a greater manifestation of His glory! The scriptures says speaking of Joseph 'until the time that his word came: the word of the LORD tried him.'(See Ps. 105:19)

Throughout all the spiritual warfare the prophetic word has tried you. God is in the process of 'making sons'. That's what it's all about making troopers. He said 'Behold, I will make thee a new sharp threshing instrument having teeth: thou shalt thresh the mountains, and beat them small, and shalt make the hills as chaff.' (Is. 41:15) We have now come through the battle as sharp new instruments for further use in the Master's hand. Triumph complete! We can say like the apostle, I fought a good fight, kept the faith and accomplished my mission. On the journey, casualty and loss were encountered but God says: I will restore to you the years that the locust has eaten, the cankerworm, and the caterpillar, and the palmerworm, my great army which I sent among you. (Joel 2:25) 'Believe in the LORD your God, (and) so shall ye be established; believe his prophets, (and) so shall ye prosper'. Blessed are all the warriors in Christ Jesus who believed! For, there shall be a performance of the prophetic words told to them because you stood fast on that word. You kept the faith. Through it all, you held on to the horns of the altar in prayer, while your eyes were watching God: AND THAT WORD WAS PERFORMED! (See 2nd Cor. 20:20, Luke 1:20)

Speak comfortably to Jerusalem, and cry unto her, that her **WARFARE IS ACCOMPLISHED**, that her iniquity is pardoned: for she hath received of the LORD'S hand double for all her sins. (Is. 40:2) God says 'I will sprinkle clean water on you, and you will be clean; I will cleanse you from all your impurities and from all your idols. I will give you a new heart and put a new spirit in you; I will remove from you your heart of stone and give you a heart of flesh. (Ezk. 36:25-26) For your shame you shall have double; and for confusion they shall rejoice in their portion: therefore in their land they shall possess the double: everlasting joy shall be unto them. (Isaiah 61:7)

APPENDIX A

New Season! A New Anointing!

…You shall go out with Joy and Peace! (Is. 55: 12)

Moreover the light of the moon shall be as the light of the sun, and the light of the sun shall be sevenfold, as the light of seven days, in the day that the LORD binds up the breach of his people, and heals the stroke of their wound. Isaiah 30:26

The LORD shall cause thine enemies that rise up against thee to be smitten before thy face: they shall come out against thee one way, and flee before thee seven ways. Deuteronomy 28:7

And I will cause the captivity of Judah and the captivity of Israel to return, and will build them, as at the first. Jeremiah 33:7

'Then shall thy light break forth as the morning, and thine health shall spring forth speedily… Then shalt thou call, and the LORD shall answer; thou shalt cry, and he shall say, Here I *am' (Isaiah 58:8-9)*

When the LORD turned again the captivity of Zion, we were like them that dream. Then was our mouth filled with laughter, and our tongue with singing: then said they among the heathen, The LORD hath done great things for them…we are glad….They that sow in tears shall reap in joy. He that goeth forth and weepeth, bearing precious seed, shall doubtless come again with rejoicing, bringing his sheaves with him. (Psalms 126)

Appendix B

WORSHIPING WARRIORS PRAY!

Men should always pray and not faint. (Luke 18:1)

But as for me, I will come into thy house in the multitude of thy mercy: and in thy fear will I worship toward thy holy temple.' (Ps 5:7)

APOSTOLIC PROPHETIC DANCE

Music along with dance is widespread and revered in our society. Commonly in our culture when we think of dancing, we think of the secular world only. In fact at one time it was considered a sin to dance, largely because people did not dance in the church. Certain denominations who have broken out of this belief, mainly Pentecostal, termed a similarity to dancing, as 'shouting' or 'getting happy'. Yet dancing before the Lord did not start with the Pentecostal church. For, King David danced before the Lord. The Bible says 'and David danced before the LORD with all his might; and David was girded with a linen ephod.' David had his loins girded up. Today's praise Dancers must put on the whole armor of God and gird themselves up with the truth. (See. II Sam. 6:14 & Eph. 6:14)

Dancing before God is an art requiring discipline of the mind, body, spirit and soul. Dancing is ministry to the Lord and has come to be called the Dance Ministry or Ministry of Dance being a relative part of the Praise and Worship Department. In Apostolic Prophetic churches the dance takes on an even higher meaning. There are Praise dancers and then there are Worshipping warriors. I also like to call them Apostolic Prophetic Wartime Dancers. In any event they certainly are Worshipping warriors who advance the Kingdom of God forth with their praise.

As I recall the first time I heard extensively about a worshipping warrior was when I met Sister Tonya. As I watched her dance, I could see a quality of spiritual warfare. In fact she displayed this gift before she became a part of the dance team. As she sat among the pews I saw her engage in a quality of warfare during worship time giving praise to God. There was something about her movement. Not just movement in the natural which is visible to the naked eye but movement in the spirit realm. A prophetic dancer has to have the ability to bring down walls like the children of Israel led by Joshua when they brought down the walls of Jericho. We as a people are naturally inclined to music, and music is such an integral part of the church that dancers and praise leaders must be careful to set the appropriate tone for the atmosphere during praise.

The believers participating in the Ministry of Dance should be on one accord. They cannot afford to operate in the flesh. They must move and dance in the spirit in order to bind the devil, shake the foundation and take down giants through their worship and praise. The dancers must take down Goliaths within and without. Along with the music the Worshiping warriors help set the tone of the atmosphere for deliverance which may come during worship, through the preached word or during the altar call. But the starting place for taking down Goliaths is with one's own attitude—one's own mindset. You can't bring down strongholds if you are bound yourself. That's why love and unity is so important.

I believe that one of God's examples of a Worshipping warrior is Deborah the Prophetess. After returning from a victorious battle, Deborah and Barak, the head of the Israel's army, began to sing a song and give praise to the Almighty God. This song was so powerful one might easily imagine that it provoked dance; but, the Bible does not tell us they were dancing. Yet, being strong in the Lord and the power of his might is a premise for an Apostolic Prophetic wartime movement whether it's in dance or other parts of ministry. (See Judges 4)

Another personification of a worshipping warrior is the Patriarch Moses. After crossing the Red sea, by the power and mighty hand of God, Moses sang a song. This song testified about God's great power! His majesty! And His Excellence! Miriam the Prophetess took a timbrel in her hand and all the women came after her with timbrels and with dances. Miriam began to sing of God's glorious triumph! When you read this passage you can just imagine the victorious warfare dance. What then is exactly the meaning of the warfare dance? The warfare dance simply means that the horse and the rider has been thrown into the sea and the chariot with the rider is no more. (See Exodus 15)

Now in our personal lives we have situations, circumstances as well as issues that we have to deal with. They are not just problems but situations God has given us to solve. We have his word and there is more than one way to war in the spirit with his word. We certainly can do warfare praying but we can also do warfare in the dance. Some songs are prophetic. As we dance before God, we rejoice because we know our answer has already been worked out. We dance a victory dance because it's already done. We see ourselves, in spirit, leaping over walls and going through troops. Indeed the horse and its rider has been thrown into the sea!

We take back territory in the spirit realm through movement including our hands and feet. And we war with our mouths filled with praise as King David said: 'Blessed be the LORD my strength which teaches my hands to war, and my fingers to fight.' (Ps 144:1) 'Let everything that has breath, praise the Lord. Let them praise his name in the dance: let them sing praises unto him with the timbrel and harp.' (Ps. 149:3) We know that victory is ours and as worshipping warriors, the victory is ours even in the dance.

Worshipping warriors not only give praise in the dance and song but in prayer. That's what makes them warriors. You cannot be an effective warrior in the kingdom of God without spending time with God in prayer. Prayer is vital to a Christian life of success. Without it you will falter. That's why Jesus said men ought always to pray and not faint. He knew if you did not spend enough time with God in prayer this life and the devil will make you faint. We don't mind worship and dance and praise as much because it involves that which is natural. That's why the world loves dance and music too. But we must pray too which does not always come so natural.

'Give unto the LORD the glory due unto his name: bring an offering, and come before him: worship the LORD in the beauty of holiness.' (1 Chronicles. 16:29) 'But the hour come, and now is, when the true worshippers shall worship the Father in spirit and in truth: for the Father seek such to worship him. God is a Spirit: and they that worship him must worship him in spirit and in truth.' (John 4:23-24) *(Excerpt from writings for the Ministry of Dance and Strong Winds.)*

References
and Suggested Books to Read

1. John Bevere "Breaking Intimidation" Charisma House, 1995, 2006.
2. Merrill and Virginia Womach "Tested by Fire" Fleming H. Revell, 1979.
3. Don Basham "Deliver us From Evil" Chosen Books, 1972.
4. Morris Cerullo "Demolishing Demonic Strongholds" Destiny Image, 2012.
5. Cindy Trimm "The Art of War for Spiritual Battle" Charisma House, 2010.
6. Juanita Bynum "Your Spiritual Inheritance" Charisma House, 2004.
7. Rod Parsley "No Dry Season" Charisma House, 1997.
8. Carlos Annacondia "Listen to Me Satan!" Charisma House, 1998, 2008.
9. Dr. Jackie Green "Spurned into Apostleship" AuthorHouse, 2006.
10. "Amanda Smith the Colored Evangelist" Schumburg Library, 1988.
11. Jarana Lee PBS documentary "The African American Church" & http://www.umilta.net.
12. Watchman Nee "The Ministry of God's Word" Christian Fellowship, 1971
13. Roberts Liardin "God's Generals" Whitikar House, 2003.
14. Judy Jacobs "Stand Strong" Charisma House, 2013.
15. Jerry Savelle "The Footsteps of a Prophet" Jerry Savelle Publications 1999
16. Dream Symbols, http://www.joshuamediaministries.com
17. Rava Zacharias "The Grand Weaver " Zondervan, 2009
18. Apostle J Brittany Woods "Comfort From Heaven"
19. Oral Roberts "When you see the Invisible you can do the Impossible" Destiny Image, 2002.

FOOTNOTES

[1] The Autobiography of Jeanne Guyon. Whitikar House.
[2] Jim Cymbalta "The Church that God Blesses"
[3] Floyd McClung "Living on the Devil's Doorstep"
[4] Dr. Rebecca Brown "Prepare for War" &
 Anna Menendez "High Level Warfare"
[5] Kim Daniels "Clean House is a Strong House"
[6] Apostle Calvin Martin " Foundation for Success:" Prevailing, Travailing and Intercessory Prayer.
[7] Jim Cymbalta "Fresh Wind, Fresh Fire"
[8] Veter Nichols "The Prayer Journey" (Dvd)
[9] Paula Price "The Prophets Dictionary"
[10] James Goll "Dream Language"
[11] John Eckhardt "God Still Speaks" & Internet source
[12] Wikipedia online encyclopedia, http://www.wikipedia.com

OTHER BOOKS AND RESOURCES

FOUNDATION FOR SUCCESS: **Prevailing, Travailing & Intercessory Prayer** is a 138 page book and text manual with reflective study questions which teaches the reader how to travail and prevail in prayer and birth the Christos apostolic, anointing to cast out demons and devils, heal the sick, heal the wounded and the broken-hearted.

11.95

4-pk CD: Prevailing, Travailing and Intercessory prayer preached by Apostle Calvin Martin. $25.00   **Individual CD** $7.00

****

STRONG WINDS: Strong Women Win. And men with standards win to. This book is an eight week study guide and journal to break up fallow ground, to heal emotions and break the stronghold of the enemy.

$11.99
Send request to Fndforlivingwater@gmail.com
Or visit online at: http://www.lulu.com/spotlight/Fndforlivingwater

$12.95
SPIRITUAL WARFARE and PRAYER: Blessed are the **WARRIORS** that **B**elieved! God is a Man 'O War and so are His sons and daughters: Warriors in the Spirit! Available from: **Createspace.com**, Amazon.com and other retail outlets.

About the Author

Debbie Jerido was born again twenty-six years ago under the tutelage of Apostle Calvin Martin at Trinity Christian Fellowship in Miami, Florida under the leadership of Rev. Joshua Bullard. At that time, she received a spiritual legacy—an Apostolic, Prophetic, Intercessory Prayer mantle. In 2005 the prayer mantle was resuscitated and launched to another level. After the call to the ministry, in 2006 the Lord led her to the company of the prophets in Michigan where she would wrestle at her own personal peniel, overcome and get the victory through spiritual warfare over a spirit of Pro-Choice. In completing the Lord's commission she was ordained as a Prophetess on Resurrection Sunday 2009 at NCLM under the leadership of Apostle Veter Nichols. Also under the apostolic leadership of Bishop James Brant, she labored in prophetic prayer for a year in the church in Detroit for the birthing of that ministry and in 2014 God birthed the church.

Prophetess D. Jerido is an author, co-author, speaker and anointed teacher on mentorship, healing, deliverance and spiritual warfare and prayer. She holds a degree in Psychology and has worked in the community, hospitals, jails and the prison system in the social services field. She has worked in church outreach areas of: evangelism, women's shelters, nursing homes, youth rallies, ministry of helps and prophetic conferences. She continues to work in these areas and continues to serve as a missionary in the community ministering to hurting people wherever God leads. She is also grateful to God to be the mother of three children and six grand-children. Prophetically proclaiming what God has said over them: Children are a heritage from the Father. Children are an inheritance from the Lord. They are arrows in thy quiver and their angels ever behold His face!

www.ingramcontent.com/pod-product-compliance
Lightning Source LLC
Chambersburg PA
CBHW060836050426
42453CB00008B/711